W9-CFW-104

MEDITATIONS FOR LIFE

BY JAMES R. DOLAN, SJ

REFLECTIONS FOR
SPIRITUAL FREEDOM

ISBN 0-9632750-5-4
0-1577256
Published by
Scotsman Press, Inc
Syracuse, N.Y. 13204

Imprimi Potest
Joseph Parkes, SJ
New York Provincial

Excerpts from THE JERUSALEM BIBLE, copyright (c) 1966 by Darton, Longman & Todd, Ltd. and Doubleday, a division of Bantam Doubleday Dell Publishing Group, Inc. Reprinted by Permission

3RD EDITION 2001, THE SCOTSMAN PRESS

PREFACE

How many people do you know who would like to become an author?

Certainly teachers, after mastering their subject for a decade or two fantasize about writing a helpful text. Most people become proficient in their field of work or endeavor and wish to share their experiences to benefit others. After reading so many books wouldn't it be great to write one yourself? That's the way I felt when I returned from India after six months with Tony deMello. My mind and heart were still charged up after Tony's inspiring program for religious formators. So I set out on the task of completing a book. I was certain I would finally put some new insights onto paper. Yaree!

After a futile four months I returned with Ignatian resignation to my favorite apostolate, giving retreats. It has always been my most enjoyable work — sharing the good news with people who had freely come away for a while to reflect and dialogue.

While directing retreats I often started each morning with a spontaneous, guided meditation. This particular retreat lasted eight days. At the end of the retreat one of the sisters, William Mary Malkoske, to my great surprise, gave me a copy of all the meditations I had presented. I could not believe what she had written nor what I had said.

Anyway, I had the first eight meditations of my new book already typed and ready for publication. It was a graced experienced, like sailing with the wind at my back - effortless. And so I followed a similar tact and the other meditations and pages unfolded as easily as if I were describing a sunset, or a rainbow, or a child's reaction on Christmas morning.

I am grateful to Kathy Mezzalingua who carefully edited the text and to Cathy O'Neil my artist friend, and of course to a dear friend Tony deMello who many years ago invited me to India - to see what I could see.

I love this whole grace idea. May you find renewed confidence and delight in these meditations.

I WANT TO DEDICATE THIS BOOK TO
YOUNG CHILDREN AND KIND ADULTS:

YOUNG CHILDREN: THEY TEACH ADULTS
THE ESSENTIALS OF
SPIRITUALITY

KIND ADULTS: THEY ASSURE CHILDREN
THEY ARE LOVED UNCONDITIONALLY.

TABLE OF CONTENTS

INTRODUCTION

This book contains a series of meditative conferences, awareness exercises, and contemplations about the love of God working in our lives. I have raised questions that can be as stimulating as the search for answers. These meditations explore issues that will lead you to respond with inspiration.

St. Ignatius' Spiritual Exercises challenge a person to think clearly and respond freely. Being in touch with one's desires, and actively putting them into action are the graces of these exercises.

If you can feel yourself being led by consolation and inspired wisdom rather than by any obligation, righteousness or competition, you are bathing in God's Graces.

The initial chapters focus on prayer and discernment. The latter meditations emphasize the challenges of today and finding God in all things.

There is a pattern of searching, disillusionment and victory in the process of the Exercises of St. Ignatius. So too with life, as we come into the world we discover all things as new; we are truly explorers. We experience the shock of life, the behavior of others and our own weakness. We find ourselves doubting, confused, isolated. Then, through the grace of God and the love of others we experience an awakening; liberation becomes a reality.

The Exercises of St. Ignatius retell the crises and passion that Jesus experienced. Jesus' personal and direct perception of life and His relationship with His Father sustained Him.

Occasionally, I have focused on the passion and suffering of our brothers and sisters today. As you identify with those who are encountering illness, tragedy and loss, may you experience the love of God and find ways of consoling and being consoled.

I have suggested a variety of contemplations with images of a God who gifts us in creation and who personally loves us. This is referred to in the final section as the "Ad Amorem."

Life would certainly be easier if you had a loving companion on your journey, especially if it were Christ. And you do! Come and see.

MATTHEW 7:8 FOR THE ONE WHO ASKS ALWAYS RECEIVES; THE ONE WHO SEARCHES ALWAYS FINDS; THE ONE WHO KNOCKS WILL ALWAYS HAVE THE DOOR OPENED TO HIM.

RECOMMENDATIONS

Treat these meditations as if they were morsels laid out on a buffet table. Take what looks and tastes good to you; this is at the heart of discernment. Many things may satisfy the heart, but frequently one thing will do it. Take one thing from each meditation and these exercises will have been worthwhile.

Allow yourself a few minutes for quiet reflection and listen to your own questions. You will make some valuable discoveries. Collecting your insights and reactions to these exercises will lead to a contemplative style in your actions.

Dialogue can deepen the concepts that are already Good News but seem too good to be true. Sharing your story will help to confirm that God's love is better than you have been taught, better than you have believed and gentler than you could ever imagine. To exchange your reflections with someone who is also praying these meditations would be helpful and stimulating. Your joys and sufferings vary, but by sharing them with a friend you are able to weave these diverse strands into the graced tapestry that God has designed.

During reflection, feel God's gentle presence within. Interior joy is like feeling favored by God. It is as if you felt thoroughly accepted and extraordinarily free. You will just have to try it.

EPHESIANS 1:13 - 14 NOW YOU HAVE HEARD THE MESSAGE OF THE TRUTH AND THE GOOD NEWS OF YOUR SALVATION; AND YOU TOO HAVE BEEN STAMPED WITH THE SEAL OF THE HOLY SPIRIT, THE PLEDGE OF YOUR INHERITANCE WHICH BRINGS FREEDOM.

1. FINDING GOD IN ALL THINGS

Discover who you are, the one whom God has made.

Exercises in awareness, practiced without strain help you appreciate the sunlight, enjoy the rain, and experience the variety of life without being overwhelmed. Enjoy one thing at a time, without worrying about things you are not doing. As you do this you will be responding to your own graces and appreciate the freedom of others and their unique decisions.

Each of us has been influenced and sometimes victimized by society. Any voices still saying, "don't trust yourself, you are not ready" or "what will people think" or "it has never been done before" are only past conditionings. These voices are not yours and not God's. You are ready - you are already free. Freedom is one thing God has called you to and promised you. The world of light is the light that God has brought into the world, into your life and into your mind.

Authority always wants you to get its approval. Yet, Jesus did not get approval from His church or from the society of His day. The world of darkness is the approval that society demands and sometimes imposes. The standards expected by society and demanded by authority are laden with praise when you conform and with rejection when you act independently. The pressure to conform and to stay in step with the herd is darkness. It is more appropriately described as "society's way" or "the world's way".

When you follow your grace you will not be able to compare yourself with anything or anyone. And you will not want to. Today's grace is different from yesterday's grace; your response to it must be a living one. And that is all that matters.

Guilt is a "should" that comes from the past, from others and from outside. Even though a "should" is something in your mind, something you are saying to yourself, it actually has its origin in some previous programming.

And so there will be some conflict when your living spirit is confronted by the authority of tradition.

In these Spiritual Exercises, let the Spirit be your Guide. The Spirit is at your center encouraging, consoling and caring. And the beauty of the Spirit is that it accepts you.

God accepts you whether you follow the desires of your heart, or whether you follow another as a lamb. There is no condition on God's love for you.

As you begin your prayer journey get into the present. Stay with the "now" and realize that God is as close to you as your heart. Periodically, listen to your own heartbeat, then feel your breathing. In this present moment God is that close to you.

JOHN 16:8 AND WHEN HE COMES, HE WILL SHOW THE WORLD HOW WRONG IT WAS ABOUT JUDGMENT.

2. NOW HEAR THIS

When you come to pray take a relaxed posture. Reclining would be the most comfortable position, if you could stay awake. Body awareness and sensitivity to your surroundings are both conducive for prayer. Once you are comfortable you will be praying before you know it.

Start with an awareness of something very simple - like your breath. It is your intimate contact with the world.

In this exercise imagine that God is completely content with you, that God has no further desire or expectation than to be near you.

God speaks to you:

"I have come that you may have life. When you were young you were the apple of My eye. When you were growing up, clumsily searching and getting lost, I delighted in your every move.

When you learned about good and evil, I recall that you felt guilty and inadequate. I wanted to pick you up and squeeze my love into you.

When you fell in love, you were so excited; you danced for joy. I danced with you.

When you had some hard knocks and felt rejected, I wanted to support you with a visible presence but I knew you would make it. I knew what I had created and I had no doubts about you.

I felt disappointed when you were taught that you could offend Me or hurt Me or lose My love. I was so sad when someone convinced you that I might punish or embarrass you.

I just want to assure you that you and I are one in mind and heart and spirit. I want you to know that nothing you could ever say or do could ever separate us: no sin, no failure, no evil, nothing in the past or future.

Even if you could reject Me I would still love you. With all of your limitations and selfishness, self-righteousness and jealousies, I have loved you with an everlasting love. I loved you when you were angry, sad, pompous or depressed. I would rather spend one day at your side than a thousand years with saints and popes and kings. I would give my life for you. I would give My son for you. I already have.

Do you know that My love has no bounds? Yes, I am always on your side and I am always at your side.

I would like to wipe away every tear and every fear you could possibly have. I am with you and I am yours always. I want you now to have a fullness of life and a deep peace that the world cannot give or take away. My covenant with you was made before you were born."

REVELATION 21:4 THEY SHALL BE HIS PEOPLE, AND HE WILL BE THEIR GOD; HIS NAME IS GOD-WITH-THEM. HE WILL WIPE AWAY ALL TEARS FROM THEIR EYES; THERE WILL BE NO MORE DEATH, AND NO MORE MOURNING OR SADNESS."

3. IF THE LORD SAYS, "YOU ARE WORTHY", DON'T ARGUE

Whenever you do an awareness exercise realize how free you are and how everything is a gift. The Spirit wants only your happiness. Your common sense deep within affirms what is best for you. Your consciousness surveys all the different gifts of the world and selects the ones that will work for you.

What does it feel like to be who you are? Do you think it would be more interesting or more exciting if you were beyond human? Do you find the challenge of being you overwhelming?

The Spirit likes you the way you are, but it is very important what you think. Prayer is like being with a person who loves you more than you love yourself.

Listen to the Spirit:

"I enjoy being with you, watching you, loving you. It is especially fun because you cannot love Me in return. Sometimes you think you are loving Me, but it is really impossible. There is no way you could thank the sun for light and warmth, or thank the trees for wood and fruit. You give Me great joy just by being with My people, just by being you.

You probably have noticed that sometimes you do carry too much baggage! I am not talking about luggage! Why are you clinging when the world is flowing?

Sometimes you realize that you have the Kingdom - that is when I see you dance. Sometimes your conditioning sneaks in and you feel that you must be the caretaker for so many, the fixer for the world, and you get over burdened; that is when I love your tears. I really love the times you share yourself.

Let us look and see what is useful for your happiness and what is not. This is all I want for you.

What is so amazing is that I have simply given you everything: space and air, rain and water, language and talents and people. And of course you have the freedom to choose which of these creations you prefer. Your particular preferences are most precious to Me. You are very easy to love when you are assertive and courageous.

When you are certain without a trace of a doubt that I love you, the next thing to believe is that I have created you to be free. You are as free as you will ever be. You are as free as anyone could be. You are as free as Jesus.

My unconditional love for you accepts you with your fears, dependencies, frustrations and weaknesses. I love to watch you do insignificant things and I love to watch you do nothing. Sometimes the less you are doing, the more aware you are of your being, which I find infinitely beautiful. Remember how happy you are when you enjoy something? That is the way it is for Me being with you! I am so happy to be with you."

LUKE 10:41 "MARTHA, MARTHA," HE SAID, "YOU WORRY AND FRET ABOUT SO MANY THINGS, AND YET FEW ARE NEEDED, INDEED ONLY ONE.

4. YOUR BREATH AND HIS SPIRIT

As you cannot cling to your breath, but let each one go, neither can you cling to the Spirit. As God gives you each moment of life, God offers you freedom to live each moment.

He loves you with all of His heart, all of His mind and all of His strength. God loves the life that He has created in you. God has no concerns about your past life or your future life. He does not keep records of the past nor forecast the future. God lives just beyond the present in the eternal now with you.

Yesterday is like a photograph, but today's breathing is God's living spirit in you. When you do not cling to your breath, you have greater life and more freedom.

God created you so that you would be like God. God sent His son to remind you that you are free and able to love just like Jesus. You have the grace of Christ. And one sign that your spirit is united to His is your breath.

If Jesus could reassure you of His love, He would whisper: *"Before you were born, you breathed your mother's breath inside her womb. I loved giving you life through her. From the very first moment when you breathed on your own, I loved giving you life. All during your life, whether you walked or drove or worked or slept, I took great delight in giving you each breath.*

One day you will no longer breathe on your own. One day you and I shall share the same breath. Any time you want a reminder of My presence, close your eyes and enjoy your breathing. I promise you, you will always have My Spirit."

JOHN 16:13 WHEN THE SPIRIT OF TRUTH COMES HE WILL LEAD YOU TO THE COMPLETE TRUTH.

5. FREEDOM IN PRAYER

I watched a child today. I watched his direct response to every stimulus that came in view. I pointed to a dazzling rainbow. I wanted him to see where my finger was pointing, but he was absorbed looking at my hand. Soon other people came and gazed at the rainbow. They "oohed and aahed" while the little child simply looked with delight at all the people making sounds. He laughed as he found himself surrounded by laughing, living, rainbows.

When a person is awake and alive, he sees all things new. Things great and small delight him. People of all sizes and shapes attract him.

Persons who are programmed observe selected stimuli and register trained responses. An adult enters a room or a church and takes his place. A child sees the same scene as a place to explore. Chairs and tables are opportunities waiting to be tapped. Candy wrappers are not regarded as carelessness on the part of a previous visitor, but as a treasure worth examining.

Many people have obligations whose fulfillment gives them satisfaction. If one's whole life is conditioned by obligations and success, then life's joy is drastically limited. For people so programmed, a very special kind of prayer is necessary: prayer without word or thought. Be absorbed by the clouds, feel the sun, the breeze, or listen to the sounds of nature. There is no appropriate place: pool side, seaside, rooftop, hilltop, private room, large chapel, city street, suburban sidewalk, field or farm is fine.

You can look at people or at one person, a butterfly or rainbow. You need to be free, to non-conform for you to be a new self. What you really need is a response to life that is uniquely your own.

Prayer is a time when there is no need for approval from anyone, when you do not seek praise from God. It is a penny, a candy wrapper, a Christmas present.

But what do you have to show for it?

Prayer is one thing you can do without measuring your achievements. Prayer is a time to be aware and to trace your reactions. It is contemplation without evaluation.

I saw a child today. I appreciated his freedom and enjoyed his thoroughly lovely actions.

LUKE 2: 29 - 31 "NOW, MASTER, YOU CAN LET YOUR SERVANT GO IN PEACE, JUST AS YOU PROMISED; BECAUSE MY EYES HAVE SEEN THE SALVATION WHICH YOU HAVE PREPARED FOR ALL THE NATIONS TO SEE."

Every author needs a muse

6. DO YOU KNOW WHEN YOU ARE PRAYING?

When you pray picture yourself as a child, for that is what you are.

A child's need for stimulus includes his eyes, hands, mouth, stomach, ears and heart. You will notice the short span of time that is needed for each of those senses to be satisfied. The child flows from one thing to the next. At times he can play with one toy for hours. He may have no trouble spending an hour eating or watching other people eat, nibbling a bit and then playing with his food. At another meal after five minutes he is ready to go. He has his own clock, his own speed, his own motor. He is a unique identity.

You will notice that a child does not cling to one emotion or idea. A child has an uncanny ability to move on, to flow with life. This is what meditation is - keeping in touch with present life. It seems as though children do it effortlessly. He holds on for a while and lets go. He says yes or no readily. The child does not hide his emotions. He responds with a miraculous appropriateness, depending on what his needs are at the time.

Can you see yourself as a child? Can you see yourself in your inspiration and response? You have unique needs for joy and satisfaction.

People search within for interior freedom that enables them to respond authentically.

Often people have been encouraged to conform rather than to contemplate. No wonder people got anxious! How often upset comes into our quiet times, into our prayer. Resistance occurs when someone is urging an unwilling subject.

When you pray, be who you are. Let the child that is in you have full expression.

When my nephew was just under two years of age, I found myself calling things by the garbled names he called them. While I could not pronounce the sounds as well as he did, it was easier than teaching him English. The names he had for things were so creative. The names reflected a connection between the child and the specific reality. Using his language gave me a special oneness with my nephew. We laughed at one thing after another. When he wanted his Mommy we found delight in searching together. It was a wholly new joy. The walk, the search and the sharing were delightfully consoling.

When you pray, realize first that you too are a child.

PSALM 103:8, 13 YAHWEH IS TENDER AND COMPAS-SIONATE, SLOW TO ANGER, MOST LOVING, AS TENDER AS A FATHER TREATS HIS CHILDREN.

Practice makes perfect

7. A LOOK AT LIFE

When you first walked out of the doors of your home and into the wide world, when you first saw groups of people in classrooms, and crowds on the street, can you remember how you felt? Was your stance one of awe and curiosity? Were you struck by the beauty and variety? Do you recall your desire to explore and how willing you were to jump in, to be part of and to accept things the way they were? There was no judgment, sadness or disappointment.

This was the time of your initiation. Whatever the age, and whatever the series of events that surrounded you, it was a strange awakening. It is ever the same.

Am I helpless? Am I helpful? Do I want to be here? Are obligations thrust upon me, or do I create my own?

We are children of the universe and children of mystery. We are members of a human family. We are closely connected members of creation and thoroughly dependent on the land, air and water. And, we are children of God. What a vocation! We are full of mystery and love. No one has ever come up with the answer to God or to life or to you. What a mystery!

Each day you start somewhere and when you look at your life you find yourself saying. What does it all mean? Who am I?" What an adventure you are living!

Was it easier, clearer and more exciting when you were a child? Do you find creation, its challenges and choices just as significant and life giving as your first childlike look at the world?

MARK 10:14 JESUS SAID , "LET THE LITTLE CHILDREN COME TO ME; DO NOT STOP THEM FOR IT IS TO SUCH AS THESE THAT THE KINGDOM OF GOD BELONGS."

8. AWARENESS IS CHANGE
WITHOUT EFFORT

Did you ever want to become someone else? Did you ever want to be different? Can you remember having desires to become "more" in some way? Why would you want to change, or become other than you are?

People act either freely, flowing from an inner source, or without freedom, driven by some outside influences. Either you do something because you want to - you choose it, or because you are coerced. Striving to win approval from God or man leads to pride or guilt. Check your motivation and see that when you were influenced by authority, reward or fear you were not acting freely. It was not you; you were not yourself.

Many people live in an unaware state. They go through their day hypnotized by stereotyped reactions. They go through their life never having lived. Their responses are heavily programmed. Their reactions are habitual rituals. They think people should be seen, subservient, obedient, conforming, and not heard.

God has created in each person a center of spirit and freedom. Your greatest joy is derived from being sensitive to God's creation. The free person realizes she is already everything God wants her to be.

Why would you want to change?

ISAIAH 44:24 THUS SAYS YAHWEH, YOUR REDEEMER, HE WHO FORMED YOU IN THE WOMB: I, MYSELF, YAHWEH, MADE ALL THINGS.

9. WHISPERINGS

Recognize the stirring of your heart from your first waking moment before you move into action. Your deepest desires often flicker and are forgotten.

Take the time to look at yourself and listen to yourself. Notice your desires today. Frequently, we live with automatic responses to the stimuli of our environment. We act like robots because "this is the way it was always done."

When you awake peruse the desires of your heart. After the previous day's activity, interaction with God's creation, after a night of rest, why not look at this information and let it penetrate your being? All of this has been stored in your heart.

Take a few moments to sort out the beauty. Take these golden moments to discover the grace you have to face the world in a fresh way.

What an interesting challenge it is to be a new creation! Seize this chance to experience it. Respond to it with a certain amount of abandon, with optimism, and with courage.

These moments of silence, reflection and fearless inventory, are the beginnings of wisdom. This is the starting point of creative action.

As you sense these deep desires, hear the encouraging whispers of God. Discover your preferences, realize your strengths and accept your limitations. Decisions will come easily. Obstacles will only add flavor to your actions and enhance the joy of your achievements.

When you realize the divine source of your desires you will not be worried about effort and measurement. You will be filled with wonder.

What a lovely start to the day! Silence, touches of acceptance and strokes of wisdom! Who could have created it?

ISAIAH 48:6 - 7 NOW I AM REVEALING NEW THINGS TO YOU, THINGS HIDDEN AND UNKNOWN TO YOU, CREATED JUST NOW, THIS VERY MOMENT, OF THESE THINGS YOU HAVE HEARD NOTHING UNTIL NOW, SO THAT YOU CANNOT SAY, "OH YES, I KNEW ALL THIS."

10. LISTEN TO YOUR CENTER

Allow your body to be quiet. Breathe as calmly as when you sleep. Slow down all activity in your mind.

Often you are distracted by your fast pace and you breathe accordingly. But during this prayer time, let heart and mind and body relax.

You often direct your heart, but let your heart direct you.

Your breath is always keeping up with you. On this occasion sense the harmony and keep in tune with your breathing. There are so many intricate paths your thoughts take, let your mind rest and allow it to reveal its deepest thoughts.

What a nice compliment it is to say to your mind, "You are quite good" and to your heart, "You are okay" and to your breathing, "You are just fine. Thanks y'all."

When you become more conscious of how faithfully these centers work for you, you will avoid breathing air that contains toxins, or subjecting your mind to things that would cause it to dysfunction. As you realize the preciousness of your heart, you will want to expose it only to life-giving stimuli. You are solely responsible for these vital centers; so listen to them, be open to them, respond to their needs and be open to change. Truth and goodness sustain them. When you are compassionate to your own heart, relationships improve, for a deeper appreciation for others develops naturally.

Realizing the beauty of this inner life, your senses awaken. You will seek clean air, constructive thoughts and compassionate ways.

So feel the peace and the ease of your breathing. Sense your heart reaching out. Feel your mind awake, and yourself full of the spirit of life.

ISAIAH 61:1 THE SPIRIT OF THE LORD YAHWEH HAS BEEN GIVEN TO ME. HE HAS SENT ME TO BRING GOOD NEWS TO THE POOR, TO BIND UP HEARTS THAT ARE BROKEN; TO PROCLAIM LIBERTY TO CAPTIVES AND FREEDOM TO THOSE IN PRISON.

11. LISTENING TO YOUR SELF

When you talk to yourself, is it a one way conversation? When you urge yourself to do something, does the urged self get equal time to respond? One of the best ways of meditating is to have a two way conversation, a dialogue with self. This will require that you treat your self as your dearest friend.

See your self as creative, up to date, as one who knows your weaknesses and gifts. One of the great things about self is that it likes you. As you have grown, it has grown along with you. When you were tired or sick, it felt the same as you did. If anyone knows how you feel, the self does. Realize that your self very much wants to listen to you. Are you also willing to listen and relate to this unique you, the you within?

The self comprehends the slightest nuance and each interpretation you express. The self is adaptable and encouraging. If what you want is in your best interest it is a hundred percent with you. And when your self is with you, you have it all together. You simply cannot fail.

To enhance your awareness of the presence of the self, make a list of the things you and the self would like to do. Make three separate columns, and list the things that you think of initially in the first column, and those that come from the deepest part of you in the second. In the third, list all the things you 'should' do. 'Shoulds' do not come from you nor from the deepest part of you. My Goodness! Where have so many "shouldy", preachy and righteous voices come from all these years? In the past, which inspirations have you heeded: the spontaneous you, the compassionate spirit or the critical voices: column one, two or three?

Maybe you felt that if you listed the things you wanted, you would be frustrated. Maybe you felt that if you made a list of what you wanted you would be considered a selfish person. So you stymied your heart's desires and you told your self, "Deny yourself, self should be seen and not heard; you don't deserve it," or words to that effect. Repression was caused by well meaning people - just like us.

This time, take care, for it is not just you that you are listening to, there is your inspired self.

Make a list of things you like and want. It will be a little surprising when you notice all your desires, the wildness of your dreams, the courage that the inner self expresses. It might take a while to uncover some of the desires that have been hidden for many years. The self did not tell you all it wanted to, because you were not ready to listen until now. This is a special meditation time to look through this powerful scope and to release whatever resides in the heart of your self.

Spend as much time as you want; you might understand better why the young are so full of wonder. What do you do with these desires of your ever faithful self? What does a child do with all her desires? How did Jesus handle His? How does God do it? Certainly you need to smile and even laugh at the breadth and the depth within you.

The best response anyone has ever come up with is: one step at a time, one person at a time, one thing at a time. Continue to pay attention to this special self that loves being inside of you. You will soon find creative ways to respond that are very gratifying and truly redeeming.

EPHESIANS 1:18 MAY HE ENLIGHTEN THE EYES OF YOUR MIND SO THAT YOU CAN SEE WHAT HOPE HIS CALL HOLDS FOR YOU.

12. BECOME AWARE OF WHAT THE
LORD HAS MADE

Close your eyes for a moment. Become aware of your breathing. Notice how your lungs naturally take just enough air. Feel your pulse. Your heart pumps life-giving energy according to your need.

Your mind also takes in as much as it wants. Sometimes you think of one thing and stay with it for a while. At other times many things stimulate you superficially. And it is refreshing when it quiets down and sleep overtakes you.

Become aware of your stomach too. It is very kind to you as it gives clear signals when it is hungry and when it is full.

There is another place inside you that is a center which sends you signals. The radar of the spirit pervades your whole body. It seems to sense right away when you are in a good place. It sends flashing signals when something is not appropriate for you.

You have such a divinely created spirit in you. It responds differently each day. As you pass a flower garden you are not quite sure with which flower your spirit will take a little leap. Your spirit is that special thing within you that selects and registers beauty. When your eyes see the moon you see color, size and shape - but when your spirit sees the moon you see beauty. When some people dance they focus on their feet. When your spirit is soaring you feel the dance throughout your body.

The spirit announces wonder and oneness. The spirit enables you to experience this unity. This spirit reveals oneness with every person, without being distracted by sickness or health, wealth, religions or cultures. "You've got the Spirit!"

EPHESIANS 4:23 YOUR MIND MUST BE RENEWED BY A SPIRITUAL REVOLUTION SO THAT YOU CAN PUT ON THE NEW SELF .

13. WHERE DO YOU FIND LIFE?

As you approach prayer today what things come to the surface first? Some days I know exactly what my intentions are, for whom I wish to pray and where I would like God to be most active. And some days I simply need to become quiet.

Sometimes it helps to ask questions: With whom would I most like to share my time? How would I design today?

It is also satisfying to look back at the end of the day to see which people brought out a fresh response from me, and where was life given and received?

What was the special combination of factors that created life in you, that made your heart skip a beat, that made you laugh, that gave you joy? Life is most meaningful when you are conscious of the many joys that are within each situation and relationship. By reflecting in this fashion you can find new perspectives before and after each day.

Through awareness, you have the capacity to find God in all things. This gift includes the ability to create and receive life.

Some find life and therefore God in very few places. Do you find God in one place more than another: in scriptural history, in the moments of each today, or in the mysteries of the future?

Surprisingly, a good exercise to find God in all things would be to select an area of your life where you have had difficulty finding God. Then ask two questions. Who first convinced you that God was not present there? If God created everything good, where did you learn to condemn things as evil? To deepen the effect of this exercise, imagine how a young child might look at the same thing. Compare your conditioned response to the reaction of a fully alive child.

Through your own reflection you will mature and once again find God in all things.

It must begin with you. What a lovely place to start!

PSALM 131:1 - 2 YAHWEH, MY HEART HAS NO LOFTY AMBITIONS, MY EYES DO NOT LOOK TOO HIGH. I AM NOT CONCERNED WITH GREAT AFFAIRS OR MARVELS BEYOND MY SCOPE. ENOUGH FOR ME TO KEEP MY SOUL TRAN-QUIL AND QUIET LIKE A CHILD IN ITS MOTHER'S ARMS, AS CONTENT AS A CHILD THAT HAS BEEN WEANED.

14. A GOOD RETREAT

What are the signs of a good retreat? If you simply enjoy the time spent, would that be good enough?

People often evaluate their prayer time by asking, "Were there good effects? Did I do all that I was asked to do?" People are accustomed to being evaluated according to how much they accomplished and how well they performed. Even the scriptures reiterate, "By their fruits you shall know them." The claim that the effects are measurably good is a relative statement. Judging and convicting depend on the standard that is used as well as the subjective opinion of the ones judging.

If God said to you, "Today, I loved watching you, I enjoyed you immensely," what a difference that would be from, "You were very productive today." It is the dramatic yet subtle distinction between love and approval.

If you trust yourself and your feelings, then the basic criterion is, "Do you enjoy your life, the choices you make, the places you live and the people you love?"

Do you enjoy what you are doing now? That is the number one question and it is yours. And God cares about your answer, for God thoroughly enjoys you, regardless of what you produce.

So when you find yourself measuring or grading yourself, slow down, take a breath, see if you can enjoy all that you are - as God does.

MARK 7:37 "HE HAS DONE ALL THINGS WELL. "HE MAKES THE DEAF HEAR AND THE DUMB SPEAK."

15. AN EXTRAORDINARY INVITATION

How would you like to receive an invitation to be singularly honored at the United Nations, the Vatican or the White House? Can you think of an honor that would exceed these? There are many worldly honors in religious life too.

What prize would make your whole life worthwhile? What single gesture could remove all the anxiety, all the pettiness, all the guilt that you have ever carried? Could God do anything for you today to prove to you that you and God are one?

This morning when you woke up there was an invitation by your bed. God invited you today to the banquet of life. All the honors you could possibly receive in this world could not hold a candle to one single day of life that God has called you to. You have been God's guest of honor from the first moment you were alive.

When you realize that you are the favorite of God, all worldly praise becomes irrelevant and the trials of the world cannot overwhelm you.

You can never earn or lose God's favor; the pressure is off. Is there anything that God could do for you to assure you?

God's love for you is eternal. Rejoice! You are God's guest of honor.

ISAIAH 55:2 WHY SPEND MONEY ON WHAT FAILS TO SATISFY? LISTEN, LISTEN TO ME, AND YOU WILL HAVE GOOD THINGS TO EAT AND ENJOY.

16. ATTENTIVE TO LIFE

Being attentive to life means you give yourself time to look at nature, to observe your relationships and to notice your reactions.

Being attentive means that you have been willing to take the time to investigate thoroughly and relying on your own graces you respond wholeheartedly.

Wisdom is the ability to suspend judgment, until you can see for yourself and discover your reaction. "Wait and see, come and see." Seeing is critical for understanding. Trust your understanding and it will guide your behavior.

Be faithful to yourself and attentive to life and you shall love and feel love; and you will be filled with joy.

ISAIAH 55:3 PAY ATTENTION, COME TO ME; LISTEN, AND YOUR SOUL WILL LIVE.

Held in the palms

17. THE REAL POWER IN LIFE

Some people find wonder in trees, mountains and sunsets. Others see it more clearly in people. Look at the marvelous things and places where children find it.

In India I met a boy named Ankush who played every day with a collapsed bicycle tire. When he hit it with a stick it would become circular and roll down the street. He brought it to life and he made it walk with him wherever he went. It was his power that made a tire walk and made my heart dance. When he let his baby brother hit the tire, it would bounce, flop and fall. More power sparkled around him as his generosity created joy and laughter.

There is a great power in you. It is brand new, yet it has always been there. Many times during your lifetime you used this gentle power. When was the last time you brought something to life, or made a heart dance? Maybe you were unaware that you were doing it. You have a power in you that is usable any time you want, whose consequences are immeasurable, whose goodness is endless. Your power is majestic.

People who do not believe in their inner power can trace the void to some induced fear or imposed commitment. People who have not discovered this interior liberating power often assume that their life is powerless and dull. They become righteous and withdrawn fulfilling their own prophesy. These people look to authority and law rather than to the power in their hearts. These deprived persons look for praise as if they could find sufficient affirmation by acts of submission.

The greatest obstacle to being who you are, to being the power that you are, can be found in examining one question, "What will people think?" Just picture yourself with an old bicycle tire, running around the grounds beating it with a stick. What would people think? You are not in control of people's thoughts. The divine question is, "What do you think?"

Opportunity after opportunity comes your way and fear blinds you from a personal response. If you could ever let your mind and heart join forces the resulting grace would bring Good News to many. Your heart has miraculous powers. It is not a dry stick that brings a tire to life. It is your very life that brings life.

LUKE 24:31 - 32 AND THEIR EYES WERE OPENED AND THEY RECOGNIZED HIM; BUT HE HAD VANISHED FROM THEIR SIGHT. THEN THEY SAID TO EACH OTHER, "DID NOT OUR HEARTS BURN WITHIN US AS HE TALKED TO US?"

He isn't heavy, he's our brother

18. HOW NEW ARE YOU?

Each morning you are awakened to the sights and sounds of new life. Can you hear them? The singing of the birds is different today. The mixture of ideas and feelings sends a unique message. You really are new!

While you are free to be true to yourself, most people have lost their sensitivity because they have been taught to be insensitive to themselves. People have had their sensitivity deadened over the years by imposed ideals, rigid habits and other past influences. If you find yourself thinking according to another's ideals you will become insensitive to the call of life. When you cease to hear the call from the creative part of you, you no longer find truth; you can no longer see God.

When you wake up, hear the call to live and respond like no one else in history has ever responded. For today is a new creation and you are a new creation. You can feel your integrity when you are true to your heart. There is no greater harmony.

Your only adequate response is one that is affectionate, unpredictable and miraculously you.

The sound of the bird is not the same as it was yesterday! The bird is new; the sound is new. You are new! Let your life be a new song.

PHILIPPIANS 1:9 MY PRAYER IS THAT YOUR LOVE FOR EACH OTHER MAY INCREASE MORE AND MORE AND YOU NEVER STOP IMPROVING YOUR KNOWLEDGE AND DEEPENING YOUR PERCEPTION.

19. MAKING LIGHT OF THE DAY

We begin certain days with positive thoughts. It can be summed up colloquially - feeling good.

Sometimes in the midst of the day we question whether we are measuring up to our previous expectations or accomplishing anything.

Some people sense a great feeling of accomplishment when they do housecleaning, others simply get tired. Some feel contentment when they write letters, others are simply relieved. Each day we notice a discrepancy between our careful plans and the limited success of our actions.

We really cannot measure ourselves by the quantity of windows cleaned, pages typed, people seen or words spoken. It would be interesting to discover whether our daily activities are continual releases from imposed pressure or a series of joys.

Sharing openly and having a moment of intimacy with another person will etch that day in the diary of our memory. One exchange can make the whole day worthwhile.

Some people get tremendous joy out of planning an event, others receive great satisfaction from understanding a past experience. What things give you joy?

As you approach an activity you become aware immediately whether you are in the mood for it or not. You feel drawn by certain things and resistance for others. The signals are quite clear and the appeal or distaste is obvious. The very things that were challenging one day can be seen as burdensome the next. Do not be surprised when your needs change. Do not let your happiness depend on the fulfillment of your limited expectations. What gives you joy is simply whatever you permit to give you joy! And the way God's grace works, it varies every day.

Your life will unfold in such mysterious ways.

GENESIS 1:16 GOD MADE THE STARS AND TWO GREAT LIGHTS: THE GREATER LIGHT TO GOVERN THE DAY, THE SMALLER LIGHT TO GOVERN THE NIGHT. GOD SET THEM IN THE VAULT OF HEAVEN TO SHINE ON THE EARTH AND TO DIVIDE LIGHT FROM DARKNESS. GOD SAW THAT IT WAS GOOD."

20. THINGS I WISH FOR

Did you ever wonder, had you been born in a different time and in different circumstances, would the path you followed be different from the one you are travelling? Do you think you might have been more courageous or more docile than you are today?

Can you imagine becoming all that you ever dreamed of and doing all the things you ever wanted to do? Maybe God could effect these changes in you.

In this exercise, change your nationality, color and religion. Change your community and your friends. Choose the age you want, the sex you prefer and the appearance you desire. Give yourself the stamina, the abilities, and the resourcefulness that would make you this new person. Admit to yourself all the desires of your heart. This will release the Spirit that God has planted in you.

In your descriptions be as clear as possible to yourself. Self-disclosure, self-admission and self-understanding are prerequisites for self-acceptance. Take your time as you uncover the enormous dreams and hopes that you secretly desire.

It will be exciting to see how far you are from realizing your goals. It will be revealing to discover that some of the things you desire already exist in precisely the form you would like them to. You will find the truth in reality, in yourself and in dialogue with others.

As you search you shall find, your prayers will be answered, and you will find what you are looking for.

JOHN 14:12 I TELL YOU MOST SOLEMNLY, WHOEVER BELIEVES IN ME WILL PERFORM THE SAME WORKS AS I DO MYSELF; HE WILL PERFORM EVEN GREATER WORKS.

21. ARE YOU ORDINARY OR EXTRAORDINARY?

You are so ordinary, how can you stand it?

Look at the ordinary things children do every day. They seem to bring life wherever they go. While a child is constantly choosing, she is not examining whether what she is doing is right or wrong. She has not yet been programmed with a standardized code for judging. When does a child begin to evaluate her behavior with the expectation of reward and the fear of punishment?

Young children are amused by life and if there is not sufficient excitement, then they make things happen. How ordinary to receive life and to give it all day long!

You can enjoy life when you are not self-conscious and you are not caught up in judgment. While this seems simple, when you can do this you are extraordinary.

If you become self-conscious you tend to get distracted from the joys of life that surround you. If you find you are making an effort, just admit it, let go, and enjoy who you are.

You are such an extraordinary person, how can you stand it?

LUKE 10:21 FILLED WITH JOY BY THE HOLY SPIRIT, HE SAID, "I BLESS YOU, FATHER, LORD OF HEAVEN AND OF EARTH, FOR HIDING THESE THINGS FROM THE LEARNED AND THE CLEVER AND REVEALING THEM TO MERE CHILDREN."

22. THE MARVELOUS SELF

The secret is confidence. The top secret is belief in self. How would you like to be in charge of your life? How would you like to be able to sort out all your desires and decide which ones will be implemented?

People who do not trust themselves would surrender control of these vast horizons of decisions to others. But for those who have self-acceptance and self-confidence, the last thing they would want to do, would be to surrender this centeredness. No one could operate you better than you.

You have a spirit deep within that reacts to all external and internal stimuli and gives direction to your life.

This lovely spirit called "self" can make wise and very personal decisions.

A person with self confidence has an uncanny patience with self. She can listen to the desires of her heart and grant them a full hearing. The centered self encourages her heart to express its deepest reactions.

We are in a very privileged position. God has created and called us to be a center. God has planted an eternal spirit within each person. Take this time to relish your unique character and charism.

You have a great vocation - to be who you are, to love yourself.

GENESIS 1:27 GOD SAID, "LET US MAKE MAN IN OUR OWN IMAGE, IN THE LIKENESS OF OURSELVES. GOD CREATED MAN IN THE IMAGE OF HIMSELF, IN THE IMAGE OF GOD HE CREATED HIM, MALE AND FEMALE HE CREATED THEM. GOD BLESSED THEM."

23. WHAT IS YOUR GOD FEELING?

The Examen was a very significant event in the daily life of St. Ignatius Loyola.

Look through your day and choose the times when you had a sense of wonder that made your heart dance. It is like a God-feeling! It is a period of reflection on today's intimate moments and on unusual personal discoveries.

Can you list today's joyful experiences? As you reflect, remember the moments of special awareness, of feeling very much alive. You may have been struck by someone's kindness. You may have had an opportunity to share your gifts. You may have had a heart to heart sharing with someone.

Imagine what it must be like to feel like God even for a moment. Try to envision having unlimited power to love everyone and everything. What a unique experience! Imagine doing exactly what you want without doubting yourself and without fear of being judged. This is a God-feeling!

Examen was a very special time for Ignatius; it gave him a very special feeling of being united with God.

God's joy is sharing wonder and compassion with people. What a shower of gifts God has rained upon you!

JOHN 8:31, 32 JESUS SAID: "IF YOU MAKE MY WORD YOUR HOME YOU WILL INDEED BE MY DISCIPLES, YOU WILL LEARN THE TRUTH AND THE TRUTH SHALL MAKE YOU FREE."

24. TRUST STARTS AT HOME

Do you trust yourself? Do you make decisions through a process of personal observation and common sense? How often do you act according to your own inspirations?

Little children react immediately to sights and sounds. When children learn that what the parent wants is truly for their good they develop a sense of their own immense value.

It is important that the child understands that what the parent wants is an obvious good and not simply a show of dominance or a battle of wills. When the child is incapable of comprehending the specific meaning of the words, the message of love and good intentions should be tangible.

The child needs to develop two levels of trust: confidence rather than confusion regarding his own observations, and confidence rather than fear in the presence of others. The child is capable of learning that there are other ways of doing things besides his own way and he will accept these alternatives if he is given sympathetic acceptance, some patient attention and an honest explanation. He will never develop this basic trust if he is manipulated into doing the parent's will. Obedience to the parent can mask a deep-seated fear.

When children begin religious instruction teachers can reinforce trust, or create new fears. If the child believes he is created out of love, he will trust himself and God. If he feels he has to prove himself by conforming to standards, fear of God and mistrust of self will be induced.

When the religious instructor teaches the truth that the child is lovable and loving, and that God loves the child, the foundation for trust is broadened. A trust similar to the one learned at home coincides with the gospel he hears in church. The outward signs of God's unconditional love explained through catechesis and scripture blend easily with the love experienced at home.

To tell a child he is unconditionally accepted by God and then threaten him with the loss of God's Grace causes scrupulosity. An emphasis on reforming one's life made many young children scrupulous.

Many adults recall from a not so distant past how religious officials taught children not to trust themselves and not to be happy with the way they were. A mistrust was developed regarding one's sexual and affectionate inclinations. Questioning traditional values was frowned upon.

We are able to understand and forgive those who taught through the use of fear and threats, realizing that they could only pass on what they themselves had experienced. They did not know what they were doing since they lived in fear themselves and were therefore incapable of reflecting or teaching the true faith. While these people would do well in the army where they must obey the will of another, they ought not to be assigned to preach the Good News of compassion.

When infallible laws are proposed as the center of one's faith rather than God's love for us, trust is ruined. How easy it was for innocent children to lose trust in exchange for the promise of a future reward and divine approval!

It is helpful to recall the significant people who loved us and who revived our belief in a God of eternal love. They have restored our spiritual life.

MATTHEW 16:12 HE WAS TELLING THEM TO BE ON THEIR GUARD, NOT AGAINST THE YEAST FOR MAKING BREAD, BUT AGAINST THE TEACHING OF THE PHARISEES AND SADDUCEES.

25. LIFE WITHOUT CATEGORIES

Who will save us from the need to be "right"?

Children were encouraged at an early stage of their development to name things accurately. When they did, they received a good feeling from authority.

Each of us has been rewarded for naming things correctly at home, school, church and work. Each of us has been programmed to have the right answers. Who can free us to become ourselves once again? Who can even show us the way? How subtle righteousness is! "Jesus, just show us the Father, and we will know the way!"

People not only wanted to be right, but developed a desperate hunger to be right. The need to be right became an addiction. Failure is devastating and even the threat of being wrong is unbearable. Righteousness and divisiveness are necessary results. How fleeting is the satisfaction derived from being right? How enduring is the emptiness from being wrong!

Does your personality change when you are with someone with "status", who is in the right place?

Society has not helped in this area. It thrives on titles and power and greed. Authority needs people who are insecure and seekers of approval. How distracting this is from eternal life, from the Kingdom of God, from enjoyment of life!

When you admit how often you judge yourself and others you may stop trying to justify your life by approval or accomplishments, and you will begin to enjoy your life immensely.

You will then rejoice wholeheartedly that God is your justification and this truth will keep unfolding, one day at a time.

II CORINTHIANS 13:5 TEST YOURSELVES. DO YOU ACKNOWLEDGE THAT JESUS CHRIST IS REALLY IN YOU? IF NOT, YOU HAVE FAILED THE TEST.

26. WHAT IS GOD'S NAME?

There are such lovely passages assigning names and titles to people, "his name shall be called John...all generations will call me blessed... Holy is His Name." I wonder what God's name is! Does love have a name? Does the one who creates all things out of nothing have an appropriate name?

It is great when parents feel inspired and name their child. Later, when the child learns to speak, she herself names everything that she sees; she gives each object and person a different name. Even though the adult repeats the dictionary name, the child preserves the name she gave it. A bird could be called "Bud", a grandmother might be called "Gaabu" and an uncle might even be called "Deebu." How original! Yet we call it "baby talk".

When we are creative enough to affectionately call God by the name that is most dear to us we become free like children. When we go beyond the title to the living meaning, then we can rejoice in the unique relationship we have with God.

I remember one time telling my nephew who was a teenager that he no longer needed to call me by the title "uncle". He said, "But I like calling you 'uncle'." When I realized how much it meant to him, I agreed wholeheartedly. It became a special sign of endearment. Another nephew calls me "Deebu". I love it.

Wouldn't it be great if children could name God as they name things and people? We would have a wonderful collection referring to the One Who is. Words similar to "Abba" would be very common. In groups we would still need a common word, a term for reference. But what is important spiritually and personally is that in our prayer we discover our own name for God. How could we find a word for the creator of everything that has happened in life, the creator of all thoughts and feelings and actions? How do we find a name for the one who has a special creative love for me?

Where do we find the wisdom, freedom, familiarity and courage? If we listen quietly in prayer we might hear a name, the one God has for me and the one I have for God.

This God who creates and chooses us is mystery, requiring no bribe or sacrifice. God is above and beyond any one church or nation.

"Loving God, You who have bestowed on us the gift of life, the glory of freedom, and the dignity of human nature, what shall we call You?"

ISAIAH 12:2, 3 GOD OF MY SALVATION I HAVE TRUST NOW AND NO FEAR, FOR YAHWEH IS MY STRENGTH, MY SONG, HE IS MY SALVATION.

Be sure to smell the flowers

27. A SENSE OF GOD

Life is like walking around looking at everything, sometimes knowing exactly what you are looking for.

Can you remember a time when you were searching for a more meaningful life? Where did you look? When you were just walking around, did you ever sense God's presence? Was it in wildlife or among the trees, in the midst of a flurry of activity, or in a quiet moment when you were alone?

Some people look for answers and meaning in one particular place. But life, like God, is everywhere. Everyone who has found truth has really found God. Everyone is surrounded by God at every moment. Why would we look in one place rather than another? Is a building that men constructed holier than the sky or the earth that God made? Could any sign be holier than a person? Where will you seek God today?

This morning I saw the sky filled with colorful clouds, with shapes and shades indescribable. And I had a touching sense of God. But then the clouds passed by and I walked on and I lost the sense of God. A little later I looked at some drooping trees and some fallen leaves. There was a collage of moist colors and I found a sense of God. The sense of wonder soon passed; and later I chatted with a friend and we shared some quality time and I found a sense of God. But soon we parted and the sense was lost again. Does that happen to you?

There are so many places to find God and so many people who give me a sense of God, yet I come and go and so do they. God is too magnificent to restrict to one place and too grand to contain in the palm of my hands. God lives everywhere in everyone, in everything at every moment.

And so our daily search is one of finding, holding and enjoying, then letting go and saying good-by - continually!

COLOSSIANS 3:12 - 14 YOU ARE GOD'S CHOSEN RACE, HIS SAINTS; HE LOVES YOU, AND YOU SHOULD BE CLOTHED IN SINCERE COMPASSION, IN KINDNESS AND HUMILITY, GENTLENESS AND PATIENCE. BEAR WITH ONE ANOTHER; FORGIVE EACH OTHER AS SOON AS A QUARREL BEGINS. OVER ALL THESE CLOTHES, TO KEEP THEM TOGETHER AND COMPLETE THEM, PUT ON LOVE.

28. YOU HAVE THE COURAGE TO BE

What great courage it takes to live each day! Life is uncertain and unpredictable. We ourselves are unpredictable, uncertain, insecure and fearful. We need as much courage to say, "Yes, it was okay" to the day that has already been, as to say, "Yes, all will be well" to the uncertainty of the day that is just beginning. Our choices will always be fallible since each day is such a new adventure.

Each person has a relative degree of freedom, whether he is confined to a house, an office, an institution, a farm or a cell. With each decision there is a core of freedom and grace that enables him to respond like no one ever has before.

You are a new creation within God's continuing creation. You have courage in the face of unpredictability, uncertainty and insecurity. This lovely courage makes life meaningful and gives refreshment to others. Go for it!

2 TIMOTHY 1:9, 10 THIS GRACE HAD ALREADY BEEN GRANTED TO US BEFORE THE BEGINNING OF TIME, BUT IT HAS ONLY BEEN REVEALED BY THE APPEARING OF OUR SAVIOR CHRIST JESUS.

29. YOU ARE SO RIGHT WITH GOD

Can you remember a time when you thought there was only one way to do things? What made you sure that your idea, way of acting, religion or vocation was right? Think of an example. In that situation did you decide for yourself or was it someone else's opinion that convinced you? If it was the latter, was the other person one who was more persuasive, one who had more wisdom about the situation, or simply one who loved you? Did the desire to be right come from yourself or from others?

The world is too varied to be categorized simplistically and to be viewed through one perspective. The mind loves to search and it shrivels up when it perceives reality through a narrow filter or from secondhand sources.

Since we all live with insecurity and uncertainty, authority's indoctrination can influence even the most gifted people. Our human susceptibility makes us vulnerable so there is a tendency to look for a master rather than for freedom. While uncertainty beckons people to look for certitude, it may cause them to look for authority rather than truth.

The beauty of searching for truth and responding with compassion is marred by the acceptance of inadequate substitutes. Our longing for God is really a deep desire for peace, truth, understanding and compassion. Idolatry, localizing God, occurs when the mystery of God is limited to selected persons, dogmas and signs. When events of history are taught as divine interventions, people are distracted from finding God in the daily loving actions of others. Consequently, people are unable to see what is truly before them. They are discouraged from thinking with open minds and from listening to their own inspirations.

God is one with creation, so do not be afraid of the world. You are already right with God, so be not afraid.

JOHN 5:24 I TELL YOU MOST SOLEMNLY, WHOEVER LISTENS TO MY WORDS, AND BELIEVES IN THE ONE WHO SENT ME, HAS ETERNAL LIFE.

30. WHAT ARE YOU STRIVING FOR?

Were you ever encouraged to 'win' in everything you attempted? Does victory consist in controlling others, conquering others or converting others? Who usually wins and what is the actual prize? Who are the losers?

In the popular novel, <u>Catch 22</u>, the standard kept changing. Is the apparent ideal never attainable? In <u>Hope for the Flowers</u>, Stripe and Yellow discovered there was nothing at the top. Do you measure up to your own standards, ones you have set, or have they been created by someone else? How realistic are your ideals? Of what value are they? Where are you heading? What do you really want in life? Is striving anything more than the desire to be recognized?

Love is not found in competition. Love does not keep record of wrongs. Love is patient and kind. Love is not anxious to be first, for one who has love has already won.

Look once again at the birds of the air, the flowers in the field and the stars in the sky.

I JOHN 4:18 IN LOVE THERE CAN BE NO FEAR, BECAUSE TO FEAR IS TO EXPECT PUNISHMENT.

31. EXAMINING YOUR DAY

Examining your daily experiences can be beneficial if the reflection is done with openness and sensitivity. Remember that it is as difficult to change your behavior as it is to discover how it became a pattern.

Which of the following seems to be an area to start: communication, diet, exercise, finances, fresh air, intimacy, location, recreation, schedule or work? Does another agenda topic come to mind?

Recall the people, places and things that are stimulating and consoling. In each part of your day you have the opportunity to create and to respond as only you can: to live and to act with a minimum of anxiety and confusion.

The inner disturbance referred to as anxiety deserves your attention and reflection. These patterns of anxiety are deeply ingrained, so patience and skill are necessary. Is a fine tuning or a radical adjustment needed?

The only change you will ever need is just letting yourself wake up and see more clearly. This awareness will lead to transformation.

Life is teeming all around you; life is waiting for you. No one could respond to it better. All this day needs to fulfill it is you.

MATTHEW 5:14 - 16 "YOU ARE THE LIGHT OF THE WORLD. NO ONE LIGHTS A LAMP TO PUT IT UNDER A TUB; THEY PUT IT ON THE LAMP STAND WHERE IT SHINES FOR EVERYONE IN THE HOUSE. IN THE SAME WAY YOUR LIGHT MUST SHINE.

32. WE TRUST AND WE MISTRUST

Some people think that the things we are anxious about are the things we love, and the people we worry about are the people we love. Once we have a definition such as that we can justify all our worries.

When you find yourself worrying about something, see if you can discover fear as the source. Sometimes I can trace the mistrust to myself, sometimes to others. At times it concerns my concept of God. When someone admits that she does not trust God it usually means that she does not trust her mental image of God, her concept of God.

If we were taught about a God who only loves certain people at certain times, our image of God became contaminated. Doubt enters the mind! Maybe God does not love all creatures, all creation, all of the time! It becomes plausible not to love myself and not to trust others.

How natural for limited human beings, who do not know God, to periodically doubt that God's love is so great that it is without any condition whatsoever! How normal it is to question that God's love for me could be boundless and eternal!

Sometimes when we encounter in creation the magnificence and grandeur of God's love, we are filled with delight and awe. At other times when we see the daily tragedies throughout the world, we are naturally thrown into doubt and we question, "How can this be? How could God let this happen? Why does God not show mercy or intervene?"

Love urges us to question and to search and to act.

MATTHEW 10:30 - 31 EVERY HAIR ON YOUR HEAD HAS BEEN COUNTED. SO THERE IS NO NEED TO BE AFRAID; YOU ARE WORTH MORE THAN HUNDREDS OF SPARROWS.

33. GUILT IS WHERE YOU FIND IT

Guilt is a feeling of uneasiness. It typically occurs when someone expects punishment. The degree of guilt and fear depends on the amount of punishment expected. When guilt becomes a chronic disease it is difficult to cure.

Since nothing a person does is perfect, guilt appears rational when one believes that every mistake deserves punishment. The feeling of guilt occurs at the moment a person realizes he has violated the explicit or implicit expectations of authority, even if the authority is himself. It is the result of personal judgment and self-recrimination. Fear is a similar feeling, but it includes the possibility of harm by someone who has the power to inflict punishment.

Some people were so programmed with guilt that it was possible for them to feel guilty not only when they were innocent of the offense, but if they happened to be in the vicinity. We must therefore examine the punisher and the punishment to find the source of guilt, not just the actual offense or the particular law violated.

We learn from mistakes; it is normal and healthy to do so. We also need to see the joy of life, the humor in our errors and not just the flaws and the imperfections by themselves. Harmony and dissonance form the glories of creation.

If someone said that you did something wrong, and you immediately felt shame or guilt, you had obviously been taught that this was an appropriate response to correction. Soon you learned how to judge and how you should feel.

Sometimes the first prayer taught to a child stated, "pray for us sinners." Each of us has known situations where the label "sinner" came before compassion. We might have been raised to believe that if someone were of a different faith, that somehow it was wrong and they were wrong. The implication was that there is one right way and we were "right". When we knew someone who did not attend liturgical services, instead of compassion, loving him as God does, we had another label for these non church-goers.

Often the first acquaintance children had with religion was the notion of sin and the idea that they were unworthy of God. Many adults still feel that an essential part of religion has to do with fear of God. We were taught to be experts in judging, yet those who stand in judgment mirror themselves and become the accused.

Since we have been taught to condemn and praise, who shall save us? The One who is to come has already taken away the sin of the world. He has already forgiven all sin for all eternity. Yet people are still encouraged to blame themselves and to feel guilt, to accuse others and to judge. What are we to believe?

Be aware of the dramatic difference between approval from authority, and love from your friend. The source for complete freedom from guilt is in someone who loves you, in someone who accepts you. To the many advocates of judgment and guilt the only response is love. This is simply the example of Jesus, the one who loved and forgave, the one who accepted the world.

Where did guilt come from anyway? Is there any reason for it now? It is very important to spend some time looking at guilt for what it is.

Ask a two year old child, "Could you forgive me for getting us lost and being late for the parade?" The child would laugh. Even a child senses the primacy of love.

The essence of forgiveness is to realize there is nothing to forgive.

COLOSSIANS 2:14 HE HAS OVERRIDDEN THE LAW, AND CANCELED EVERY RECORD OF THE DEBT; HE HAS DONE AWAY WITH IT BY NAILING IT TO THE CROSS.

34. THE IGNORANCE OF FEAR

What kind of day will it be today? It seems like the day was waiting for me by the time I awakened. I wonder how people will relate to me today? I wonder if it will be a productive day? Will today be boring, anxious, or quiet? Do I sense any fear or worry?

How do I look at life? Do I see it as though I were peeking out at a strange and overwhelming world, or do I feel one with it?

Primitive people had many dangers to worry about: avalanches and unpredictable storms, marauding tribes and feared strangers. Like the poor, they struggled to make their lives secure in the midst of ongoing insecurity.

People originally thought that God sent rain as reward or punishment (whichever seemed more appropriate). Churches professed that they were divinely inspired with the right to rule. The common people had to contend with powerful inherited beliefs about the authority of the government. Individuals needed extraordinary courage before they would have the audacity to dissent.

During the Enlightenment Era, God was removed as the direct source in nature and as the supporter of man's institutions. When images of God intimidate people it is time to renew the image of a loving creator. Yet the notion of a vengeful God dies a slow death.

Many people today are still very fearful. What is the cause of this fear? God is unknown and unknowable, and fear is an emotion that is unintelligible. When people express what they mean by "fear of God" they refer to the 'beliefs' they were taught, fear-inspiring beliefs like fear of a future judgment by a condemning God. In terror many people resort to being observant, righteous and critical of themselves. They think if they judge themselves they might somehow avoid some terrible judgment. In so doing they have already been judged.

How can one become recreated and escape this fear totally?

First, it is good to see clearly that fear is exclusively in the memory. Second, it has been programmed there by others. It did not come from life; and in no way did it ever come from God. Third, wisdom and grace enable us to overcome fear as we come to new understandings of the mysteries of life, just as light dispels the darkness. Fourth, the opposite of fear is love: God's love for us and our love for one another. We are able to give our very life in spite of the risks.

If you put these reflections into practice you will have no reason to fear.

I CORINTHIANS 13:4 - 7 LOVE IS ALWAYS PATIENT AND KIND; IT IS NEVER JEALOUS; LOVE IS NEVER BOASTFUL OR CONCEITED; IT IS NEVER RUDE OR SELFISH; IT DOES NOT TAKE OFFENSE, AND IS NOT RESENTFUL. LOVE TAKES NO PLEASURE IN OTHER PEOPLE'S SINS BUT DELIGHTS IN THE TRUTH; IT IS ALWAYS READY TO EXCUSE, TO TRUST, TO HOPE AND TO ENDURE WHATEVER COMES.

35. YOU HAVE NO MORE EVIL TO FEAR

Sufficient for the day is the fear thereof! While we are exposed to dangers, rough roads and losses, each day has secure, restful and joyful moments. Each day presents certainties and unknowns. To avoid the stumbling blocks we need guidance from people who have travelled before us.

People who show us the way have their own biases, so as we listen to their experiences we must come to our own understanding.

Some people have been taught to feel guilty. Others have been taught to be afraid of immaterial things, like the future, the next life and God, and to be suspicious of things that bring pleasure, like possessions, relationships and love. How many people do we know who are afraid of failing, or of what others will think, or of being overlooked? Our growth was stunted if we were taught fear rather than awareness.

We find people walking through life not in touch with the delights of life but only with a series of cautions. To see exclusively through the filters of what authority has taught, brings a person to a subjugated level similar to an animal whose instinct is its only authority. Instead of responding to life, the fearful person projects illusory thoughts of threatening situations and then reacts emotionally to these thoughts. This emotional reaction is called "worry" in minor occasions, "fear" in major cases, and "panic" in dramatic situations. Fear and worry do not further understanding, but do cause many thoughtless actions.

Each day we are called to respond in a variety of ways. To each of these thousands of gentle calls rather than responding as confident sons and daughters of the Lord, we often are obsessed with hesitating questions: Will I be justified? Will I be rewarded? How will others see me? Will I be accepted? This layer of conscience and this screen of approval constantly coat our actions with fear.

Fearful people are filled with apprehensions about the most insignificant things. They feel responsible for a future that never occurs. Their habitual motivation resides in their conception of what others might think. And so, their actions become tenuous. The slightest decisions become magnified and psychic energy is drained. Worry becomes visible in their demeanor, their facial expressions and their hesitant behavior. They are not satisfied with the day that the Lord has made, nor have they accepted their participation as either graced or adequate. As a result, they experience failure and feel judged without any visible cause.

But fear by any name, religious or secular still causes minds to be distracted, hearts to be anxious and behavior to be compulsive.

Notice the things that you are still afraid of. How frequently do these objects of fear present themselves? The source of them will be found in yesterday's behavior and tomorrow's judgment. Take on awareness in the present and you will take on life without fear.

Can you imagine a bird who is afraid of flying or a tree that is worried about blossoming? The filters through which people see life may be tinted with fear. To drop your fear, clean the windows, get new lenses: see for yourself.

ISAIAH 43:1, 2 DO NOT BE AFRAID FOR I HAVE REDEEMED YOU; I HAVE CALLED YOU BY YOUR NAME, YOU ARE MINE. SHOULD YOU PASS THROUGH THE SEA I WILL BE WITH YOU; OR THROUGH RIVERS, THEY WILL NOT SWALLOW YOU UP. SHOULD YOU WALK THROUGH FIRE, YOU WILL NOT BE SCORCHED AND THE FLAMES WILL NOT BURN YOU.

36. THE SELFISH ARE FEARFUL

Do you remember the last time you were selfish? Do you recall anything you were afraid of that may have caused this behavior?

It is natural to be afraid of losing what you have, or what you want. Unhealthy selfishness is noted by fear and sadness: fear of losing something and sadness because they are fearful.

Healthy people are selectively selfish. People who are generous share their time and ideas as well as their personal items. It is as though their possessions are the least of their many gifts.

A musician who shares her song does not diminish her talent, if anything she increases it. The same thing happens in loving another. In a mysterious way by giving away our gifts there is an increase for the giver as well as the receiver. It might be good to look over your gifts and possessions and see if you can locate any you are afraid of losing. If you realize that you cannot lose, you will discover that sadness disappears.

Here are some considerations to confront your fear. First, ponder the fact that you are the child of the King, and you are an inheritor of the kingdom for now and always. Second, there is no way that you could ever lose the grace of God. No power in the world, nothing in life or in death could ever lessen the Spirit of God within you. If you could verbally reject all the traditions of all religions and all the images of God passed on to you from books or people, you would still not be separated from the kingdom. Recall the lovely Isaiah passage of God's promise of love, "Yet even if these forget, I will never forget you." Isaiah 49:15

People were taught that if they were independent and selfish, they would lose the favor and the love of God. This untruth has threatened people and instilled fear. The result has been protracted spiritual blindness for many of God's adult children as well as His little ones.

The source of selfishness comes from a belief that you could lose it all. You can never lose it! You were created by the Love of God, you cannot be unloved. Let no one convince you otherwise.

Ponder your own experiences of caring, sharing and of letting go. Recall how your generosity was rewarded and how the immediate experience was consoling. Generosity is an awesome mystery. It is as beautiful and as simple as a child sharing his cookie. Generosity is joyful, nourishing and courageous. But you cannot be generous if you are afraid of losing. So ponder any fear of loss and realize you can never lose. We have His Word on that.

PSALM 91:5, 15 YOU NEED NOT FEAR THE TERRORS OF NIGHT, THE ARROW THAT FLIES IN THE DAYTIME. I ANSWER EVERYONE WHO INVOKES ME, I AM WITH THEM WHEN THEY ARE IN TROUBLE; I BRING THEM SAFETY AND HONOR.

My whole life is a prayer

37. GUEST OF HONOR

Can you remember in early childhood entering a room where everyone stood in awe of you? Can you still hear the compliments? Do you recall hearing them speak about you in delightful terms as they admired your facial expression, the particular outfit you were wearing, your beauty? Can you recall their glowing remarks about your accomplishments? Can you recall the anticipation on their faces as they hoped you would crawl closer to them? Do you remember their joy when you let them touch you or you reached out to them?

Some people are able to continue experiencing their own value even when they are lined up in classroom desks like tomato plants in a garden. Certain individuals have retained the perception that they are special.

I wonder how many times Jesus had center stage and how often he shared it with others! Whenever He went to someone's house, do you think Jesus was the center of attention, or did He use this opportunity to let another's light shine?

In order to accept others we must sense our own value. One who is self-confident can sincerely praise another. To be able to say "I am sorry" requires the gift of knowing I am okay myself.

From the first moment that God called you into life you have been by nature and grace, by design and promise an eternal guest of honor.

Had you forgotten who you were? Did someone not recognize your status? Did the number of people in schools or pews distract from the truth and beauty of your centeredness? Any experience that distracted you from the truth is like a cloud that hid the light of the sun. The light is still there; it is still yours. And people who have seen the light cheer your coming and praise your least accomplishment.

If you let yourself believe that you are the "guest of honor", you will find it easy to treat others as Jesus did. You will experience their dignity without the slightest jealousy.

Your limelight is big enough to share with the world! Sometimes it is as gentle as the morning star, sometimes it is as lovely as the moonlight, at other times as bright as the sun.

Welcome, invited guest! Welcome, chosen one!

LUKE 3:22 AND THE HOLY SPIRIT DESCENDED ON HIM IN BODILY SHAPE, LIKE A DOVE. AND A VOICE CAME FROM HEAVEN, "YOU ARE MY SON, THE BELOVED; MY FAVOR RESTS ON YOU."

I look confident because my brother is driving

38. THE SEARCH FOR ORIGINAL ACCEPTANCE

Quite naturally, children seek happiness, satisfaction and things that please them. By crawling, walking, by putting all kinds of things in their mouths, and by touching everything, they explore the world. It is as if the whole universe is their turf. They always seem so surprised when something does not respond to them peacefully. They are always astonished when the dog they are playing with bites them, or the head whose hair they are pulling makes an "ow" sound. They are shocked when the dresser drawer they are pushing catches their fingers. Children are naturally surprised, delighted and hurt by life. Initially, they react to life without a conscience. They are constantly responding on the basis of whether something pleases them or displeases them. The healthy child is definitely the center.

When did you finally believe that you were justified by God's love, by Christ's love, by the Spirit of love? How often do you convince others of their original acceptance?

If people judge you and you do not judge them in return, their judgment flows by as though it were air. But when you dwell on the remarks that people make about you, before long you in turn are judging.

When children are corrected at an early age, they let critical statements pass. Later, instead of enjoying activities for their own sake, they begin to measure themselves. This transfer from self-confidence to the need for external confirmation is due to constant praise and criticism that wears them down.

When a child internalizes these judgments the conscience of society and family is imbedded in the child. Thereafter, life is measured by, "Should I or shouldn't I?" Judgments are based not on ability, joy or preference, but on permission. The question becomes, not so much will I be hurt or happy in life but, will I be approved of or punished by members of society, will I be regarded as good or bad?"

A religious conscience fits in well with someone who has already been programmed by home and society. A religious woman can feel she is good or justified if she does the 'expected' thing, if she conforms to community or church rules. Reciprocally, if she breaks any regulation she senses an immediate emotional jolt called "guilt" - she judges that she has not measured up to some "should".

Guilt is a feeling of self-rejection. Even if there is no judge present, the person still feels convicted. And although there is no visible punishment the inflicted emotional pain is real.

There is a normal tendency in every person for justification and for acceptance. Children as well as adults prefer to have others' approval. But in some organizations permission is required for each and every communication and activity. Those who have no self-confidence need to know which actions will be praiseworthy and which ones are subject to criticism or liable to punishment.

Frequently, the desire for personal freedom expressed in open dialogue is viewed as a real threat to the established order. While the military and some churches, governments and businesses still operate that way, this is not life; this is never life giving.

Jesus accepted the world. He did not come to judge, condemn and convert it. Once people realize they are loved unconditionally they will no longer hunger for external verification. They will already believe "The Good News". They will return to their true vocation - being children of the kingdom believing in their own eternal acceptance.

MATTHEW 23:4, 11 DO NOT BE GUIDED BY WHAT THEY DO: SINCE THEY DO NOT PRACTICE WHAT THEY PREACH. THEY TIE UP HEAVY BURDENS AND LAY THEM ON MEN'S SHOULDERS, BUT WILL THEY LIFT A FINGER TO MOVE THEM? NOT THEY! THE GREATEST AMONG YOU MUST BE YOUR SERVANT.

39. YOU HAVE BEEN CHOSEN TO LIVE TODAY

God loves you. There is no more dramatic and yet simpler sign of God's love than the fact that you are invited to life itself. Of the many honors you could imagine no invitation could be more inspiring than the one already offered to you to be alive and active this day.

As enormous clouds pass overhead, as you inhale each breath, as you see streets, buildings, trees, and the flurry of people, you have been given a grand invitation to observe life in all its detail, in all of its splendor. You can be aware of whichever things you wish, and taste a variety of creation. How exhilarating this realization is! Can you hear yourself say, "What more could I want in life?"

There is vivid life but no urgency. To be able to relax at table is a clear sign of peace. To be able to walk leisurely is a sure sign that there is no fear.

This world is your home! With all of its strangeness, originality and undiscovered treasures, this is all part of your unfolding inheritance.

A child will climb out of his crib, look at all the stimuli and opportunities surrounding him and ponder, "Shall I jump in Mommy's bed? Shall I explore the kitchen? Shall I play with one of my toys? Shall I make some noise so I get some attention?" Your adult choices are similar. This is your day to explore, to respond, to recline, to make some noise, for God has loved you into life.

ISAIAH 9:1 - 2 THE PEOPLE THAT WALKED IN DARKNESS HAS SEEN A GREAT LIGHT; ON THOSE WHO LIVE IN A LAND OF DEEP SHADOW A LIGHT HAS SHONE. YOU HAVE MADE THEIR GLADNESS GREATER, YOU HAVE MADE THEIR JOY INCREASE; THEY REJOICE IN YOUR PRESENCE AS MEN REJOICE AT HARVEST TIME..

40. SURPASS YOURSELF

Did you ever try to be other than what God made you? Isn't that a funny thought? It was even funnier when you tried to accomplish it. When you try to change what you are or improve reality, your behavior becomes absurd.

Just as institutions have plans for their members, you naturally have ideals and dreams for yourself. Straining and striving for ideals are not Godly endeavors, but actually man-made endeavors. It is a form of conditioning that takes away the beauty and spirit from life. The only joy in musing about changing yourself is the fantasy itself.

Can you remember parents or teachers who wanted students to become "more" than they were? They are called, "If" teachers. They would use phrases like, "If you tried harder, if you would do this, if you would only..." With apparently good intentions they projected all kinds of possibilities. They were often able to get you to focus on their expectations. Look at the formation programs organizations require of their members. Destructiveness occurs when a formation program takes precedence over the candidates themselves.

When you put pressure on yourself and others to accomplish goals set by others, this learned behavior becomes a mode of operating. You become habituated to look beyond people, hoping for a greater self, and in the process you no longer see and accept yourself.

How do you separate the idealism and expectations residing in your concepts from the reality that God created and that really exists? It is amusing when you think of all the things that you are capable of and that you could potentially do. It would be amusing to list all the possible places you could visit in the entire world. However, you are here and if you went some place else you could not be here, and if you became someone else you could not be you.

Sometimes the pressure does not come from authority's expectations but from peers or siblings who hunger for control. When people are mistreated, they feel inadequate and lose interest in taking care of themselves. Consequences may include scrupulosity, cynicism, burnout and depression. Without realizing it we can do to ourselves the very thing that we had hoped to avoid.

When the seductive trap of non-acceptance is set, the lack of confidence causes confusion and manipulation.

Joy is severely limited in three ways. First, you do not see yourself as you are. Second, you are so directed at measuring up to higher standards that you are not satisfied with the you whom God creates now. Third, discontent prevents you from noticing the joy of the present moment, and life's treasures that surround you go undiscovered. What can you do about it?

The secret is in God's acceptance of you. The secret is in your daily acceptance of the things that you are and do. This realistic belief in God's daily acceptance of you is greater than all the potentials and all the possibles.

There is a great high in store for you, not only for the future. The greatest high is in today. If you become quiet maybe you can hear it or feel it. If you close your eyes maybe you can see it. If you let go of your great expectations, you might discover that you do little things quite beautifully.

Fortunately, you cannot be other than what God made you. How wonderful!

EPHESIANS 3:12 WE ARE BOLD ENOUGH TO APPROACH GOD IN COMPLETE CONFIDENCE. SO NEVER LOSE CONFIDENCE JUST BECAUSE OF THE TRIALS; THEY ARE YOUR GLORY.

41. EVERYTHING GOD CREATED IS OURS

How exhilarating it is to be alone with the immense sky overhead! What a magnificent feeling to stand in solitude before the vast sea, with sandy beaches and sea formed coasts! It is invigorating to see the light of day, to take time to feel the air and experience peace of mind.

We feel insignificant next to the cosmic spirits of endless sky, level seas and rugged land, yet somehow we feel one with this grand expanse.

It is stimulating to be near other people who are sharing the same thing. It is easy to see why God wanted others to share in creation. God brought us into existence so we would appreciate fully without possessiveness. There is no need to be jealous or envious, covetous or clinging; there is enough for all.

It is natural to desire, to ask for and to enjoy material things. There is great joy in having and holding, and another level of joy in freely letting go and sharing with another. There is an exceptional delight in seeing the joy of others.

Which gives greater pleasure, having or letting go, when someone holds on to you or when they let go? Which is more satisfying, nightfall with its restfulness, or daybreak with the sounds of life? Let us enjoy the night and the day, let us enjoy the sky and the earth and the water. Let us enjoy the holding on and the letting go, the rising and the falling, the increase and the decrease of life. Let us appreciate fully birth and death.

God has called us to be aware, to appreciate and to experience intimate joy.

Unhappiness is often caused by a craving for things that are not available, for things we are unable to achieve. It occurs when we are not satisfied with who we are today or what is ours now.

If children are deprived at an early age or if they get the impression that what belongs to their parents is not theirs, a craving is instilled; they feel that they never have enough. They feel short-changed by life. When children are not allowed sufficient time to hold on, they never experience the freedom of letting go. It is very difficult for them to discover that the freedom of letting go is really as lovely as the security of holding on. While the beauty of welcoming provides great joy, letting go, saying good-by and moving on offers a special kind of happiness as well. It leaves a person richer, happier and freer.

The clouds come toward us and float by; there are no regrets. The sky at times is white and blue and then amber, grey and black. We learn to appreciate each in turn.

God has created sky, water and earth for people to partake, without greed and without violence. This is God's benevolence to us and God is present in these gifts.

Everything in the world belongs to us. And wonder of wonders, we belong to each other.

JOHN 1:16 INDEED, FROM HIS FULLNESS WE HAVE ALL RECEIVED. YES, GRACE IN RETURN FOR GRACE.

42. CHRIST HAS REDEEMED US IN THE PRESENT

Once people realized they were raised on promises, they understood why they kept looking to the future. These young people were so bribed with promises that finally they were distracted from living life!

Remember the times when you hoped for things? When you were healthy, satisfied, thinking clearly and free, you did not need them. You did not need extra assurances.

Usually you succumbed to the seduction of promises when you were feeling down and vulnerable. That's when promises always seem attractive.

When you hoped in the future, did you realize that you were not accepting the present life the way God made it? Somehow you renounced the present and found yourself gazing into the future.

When someone said, "Give up the present goods of this world; give up the gifts of God at this present time and give up the joys of your heart and your reward shall be great at some future date," it sounded appealing, in some masochistic way. We were indoctrinated well, because what we believed we passed on to others.

No one in his or her right mind would purchase an insurance policy that was not redeemable. Some people believe that real life will happen after life. In order to have believed that, you must have been emotionally damaged and radically deprived, especially when you have the words of Jesus, "Eternal life is now... The kingdom of God is here... Look at the birds of the air... I came that you may have life..."

What is it that makes you so subject to the will of another, so capable of rejecting yourself, so susceptible to the allure of gambling your life? Can you find the characteristic in you that has led you to look for life, not in present life, but in future death? What motivated you to look for life in authority's ambiguous promises?

For many of us, the reason why we are so susceptible is because we were taught to be afraid. And we learned it well. With all the things that nourish life, our minds have been burdened by fear rather than sustained on healthy nourishment.

I have met children who are afraid of teachers and teachers

who are afraid of students. I have met workers who are afraid of employers and parishioners who are afraid of priests, sisters who are afraid of people in their own community, parents who are afraid of their parents.

What are you afraid of? Of all the beauty, goodness and variety that God creates every day, do you find fear, or do you see truth?

Insofar as you experience fear and anxiety in your life, you will find yourself longing for relief. You will find yourself looking for a bribe, a promise, anything to substitute for real life.

How can you believe that all the promises that the Lord has made are for you to see now? Today is the promise fulfilled in your midst, in your hearing. The Lord is with you. His Word has become flesh.

Why look to the heavens? Why look to the future? The Way, the Truth and the Life is here and can never leave you.

JOHN 1:3, 4 THROUGH HIM ALL THINGS CAME TO BE, NOT ONE THING HAD ITS BEING BUT THROUGH HIM. ALL THAT CAME TO BE HAD LIFE.

43. A BASIC NEED

There you go again, worrying and fretting about so many needs; and yet there is only one. Of all the things you could dream of or hope for in this world, there is only one basic need. If you had God's love you would have everything. And you have God's love! Full stop!

Since you are distracted by activities, thoughts and desires, you unconsciously overlook the fact that your only necessity is already fulfilled. On certain occasions when you had forgotten this truth you developed unfounded fears. How did you rebound and content yourself with the joyful knowledge that you have God's love? Did you talk to a friend? Did you take a walk and observe nature? Did you become still and read something inspirational? Did you recall the times that God has taken care of you?

If we could be sure that there is only one thing necessary, we would be able to find it, believe it, and rejoice in it. But we get distracted by our desires, our efforts and goals, by other people's words and silences, and by their actions and omissions. We find ourselves wanting something to happen, or someone to accomplish something. We have a multitude of desires within us. And actions, things, people and desires distract us from noticing that only one thing is essential.

In the story of Mary and Martha in Luke's tenth chapter, Martha could have been thrilled that Jesus was visiting. She could have felt privileged to serve. The Lord had visited her, stayed at her house, enjoyed her hospitality, yet she did not realize that the only thing she ever desired she already possessed. He was here - in her own home - with her. What distracted her? What expectations could possibly have kept her from realizing that she was serving the Lord?

What things distract you so easily? Many times, besides being grateful and joyful we want more. We want attention, praise, appreciation. How normal! And yet how distracting from the joy that we already have!

How often do you enjoy preparing, working, playing and serving? And then something distracts you and you feel the absence of joy.

How easily we can become distracted even when we have the whole kingdom around us! It is so wonderful to realize that you have the one thing necessary for your life. Amidst all the diversions, you have the Lord's presence and love. It is so gratifying to remember that you can never lose God's love.

Do you have a special way to remind yourself that you have God's Spirit?

LUKE 12:25, 31 CAN ANY OF YOU, FOR ALL HIS WORRYING, ADD A SINGLE CUBIT TO HIS SPAN OF LIFE? IF THE SMALLEST THINGS, THEREFORE, ARE OUTSIDE YOUR CONTROL, WHY WORRY ABOUT THE REST? SET YOUR HEARTS ON HIS KINGDOM AND THESE OTHER THINGS WILL BE GIVEN YOU AS WELL. THERE IS NO NEED TO BE AFRAID LITTLE FLOCK, FOR IT HAS PLEASED YOUR FATHER TO GIVE YOU THE KINGDOM.

44. ONLY THE FREE CAN LOVE

What do you want from life? People who must please every-one and those who must do what they are told do not have interior peace. Those who live under a strict religious or political regime feel restricted and their hearts cry out for freedom.

When we give control of our behavior to another person, we have lost something precious. People who think they will find peace by following an authority are cruel to themselves, because obedience without personal choice is slavery. In an apparent effort to please others, they deny themselves. This conditioned abuse is difficult to escape from.

The sacrifice of freedom is too great a price. For the loss of freedom removes the mastery of one's will and the ability to love. By living in fear of another person I destroy a priceless treasure God has given to me. No government, institution or religion has a right to take away this inherent gift.

God did not create us to be fearful of others nor to be cruel to ourselves. It is against the nature of human beings to be subject to another's will, to be slaves.

When people are more concerned about another's opinion than they are about their own true feelings, they find it very difficult to recognize God in their lives. Those who do what others say, in order to be praised, are prevented from experiencing the joys of life. Those who try to measure up to the standards that others have set live in constant fear of rejection.

What do you want from life? If you are confident in God's love for you, the exercise of your freedom will enhance it. To enjoy that independence fully, realize that no one can give you greater permission than God's acceptance. You are not anyone's master, nor is anyone your master. This is the message of Christ.

Admittedly, if you use your freedom, there is a price to pay. When you find your treasure, it involves giving up many things that the world holds dear. You will discover that you no longer need affirmation from people in power nor will you rely on the worldly signs of success.

Freedom, while always delightful, is a struggle and a challenge, and you will sometimes find yourself checking to see if you chose the right path. Since human nature is fallible you will occasionally wonder if the security of permission and the dependency on approval are still viable alternatives.

Your spiritual journey includes a daily leap of faith, for you do not know the way. But the cherished dance of freedom is well worth it.

What do you want most from life? You have it.

ROMANS 8:15, 16 THE SPIRIT YOU RECEIVED IS NOT THE SPIRIT OF SLAVES BRINGING FEAR INTO YOUR LIVES AGAIN. THE SPIRIT HIMSELF AND OUR SPIRIT BEAR UNITED WITNESS THAT WE ARE CHILDREN OF GOD.

45. TODAY IS DELICIOUS

How did you enjoy the meal? How did you enjoy the book? How did you enjoy today? How did you enjoy the last hour?

When a priority has been placed on the successful completion of a task we find ourselves anxious to accomplish each thing. Life itself becomes something to complete.

Some people are actually living for the day after this one. In religion class, people spoke of the kingdom as if it were a future goal achieved at the end of life.

One day a friend of mine had eaten a lovely dinner very quickly. I asked him how it tasted. He answered, "Why, was there something wrong with it?" He had no notion of the different flavors, textures and tastes. Unconsciously, we do many things without being aware of what we are doing. How often are you attracted by some end result or future benefit?

How sad it would be if a florist did not enjoy planting the seeds and watching the flowers bud and blossom! What a tragedy if his joy occurred only when the flower was sold, when the plant was gone! We have been conditioned to find joy not in the ball game but only when the final score is recorded. We have been seduced by concepts. Unhappiness is the inability to appreciate the miracles that occur every day. Happiness is not found in the aftermath of accomplishments, but in life itself.

Some of us have been conditioned to be dissatisfied with anything unfinished. People have been conditioned to have great expectations, big appetites and "rational" greed. When people are sufficiently unhappy, they will seek a solution.

Why precisely are we dissatisfied with ourselves? The first place to look is at assumptions. Grand expectations are a common cause for disappointment. The second thing to examine would be enthusiasm. If your heart is not in a thing or if you are not thoroughly interested, you tend to get tired quickly. Third, establish realistic priorities for the present and the future. Do not let focusing on the expectations for prosperity cause you to miss the grandeur of the present.

How difficult it is to live in the present, to rejoice in who we are and to feel the singular celebration of this day!

Spend extra time enjoying what is, rather than anticipating what is not. You will have an abundance of energy. Distractions and fear will be a rare occurrence. Keep it simple. Turn on the light, adjust the shade, feel the water, taste the food - experience life.

How is the book? How is this moment? Did you enjoy the last hour? Live it to the full, taste it - delicious! God, it is delicious!

EPHESIANS 5:9 NOW YOU ARE LIGHT IN THE LORD; BE LIKE CHILDREN OF LIGHT, FOR THE EFFECTS OF THE LIGHT ARE SEEN IN COMPLETE GOODNESS AND RIGHT LIVING AND TRUTH.

46. WHERE ARE YOU LOOKING FOR THE KINGDOM?

Some people think that the kingdom will be found in some altered state or future time. Others believe that the kingdom of God is within.

Those who think it is in the future are cautious and careful, waiting for the kingdom to be revealed. This world with its enormous poverty, inequality and injustice, does not resemble a kingdom by any standards. It would seem fair to assess that the kingdom must be in the future.

Certain people feel that the kingdom is something they themselves are responsible for. They feel that if they work hard enough, if they keep striving, they will gain the kingdom. The pace gets a bit feverish at times as people are tugged hither and yon by some energetic soul, albeit depressed, who says that the kingdom of God will be achieved if specific works and rituals are performed. These people are driven; their desire for success distracts them from realizing their oppressive tactics and justifies the damage inflicted on others.

The kingdom is future to the extent that today is yesterday's future. And the kingdom can only be earned to the extent that in order to see the glorious sunrise we need to look east early in the morning.

Another class of people believes that the kingdom of God is here and now and within. They feel it cannot be comprehended, earned or deserved. They are slow to speak of God except as mystery. They do not feel responsible for converting people to their beliefs. They readily find God in others, regardless of religious affiliation, race or national origin. Such people are generous because they realize they cannot lose the kingdom. They share their time, their possessions, their thoughts, even their lives. These people cannot be manipulated because they are not obsessed about salvation nor threatened by a belief in a future judgment. These people walk among the living, see a lot of life and possess ongoing happiness.

The first two classes of people derived their beliefs from others and they are often guilty or neurotic. The third group of believers comes to their awareness through grace.

Where do you find the kingdom?

ROMANS 14:8 IF WE LIVE, WE LIVE FOR THE LORD; AND IF WE DIE, WE DIE FOR THE LORD, SO THAT ALIVE OR DEAD WE BELONG TO THE LORD.

A Rose In December: Dorothy Kazel, OSU

A Rose in December: ITA Ford, MM

47. HAPPINESS IS IN THE SEARCH

Seek and you will find. Jesus was always giving ways to happiness. As seeing fills the senses, so awareness fills the heart. Slowing down enables us to feel the pleasure that the world gives.

Joy comes from our ability to experience beauty and wonder. By enjoying nature, we are very much like God who loves creation and creates out of love.

The world's style, society's pressure and our achievements do not satisfy our hearts, but in fact create greater needs, stronger appetites and greater dissatisfaction. Jesus said ask, search, and knock, but He did not want us to be anxious. Rather than waiting to become perfect, or waiting for peace in the world, He wanted us to be fully active and to enjoy our relationships, our discoveries and our labor.

We have been raised to be productive. Yet, what do we have to show for our input? What have we accomplished? Many of society's requirements, school's demands and church's expectations have only provided structures for law and conformity. The illusion was that we would be happy if we did what we were told to do. We might attain some of the institution's goals if we obeyed, but not happiness. That is not society's domain; it is exclusively God's gift.

Children just love to ask questions. They enjoy their thoughts and what they are saying; they enjoy talking and they love getting your attention. When children ask questions, wise adults realize that literal answers are unnecessary. Their joy does not depend on the answer.

Jesus asked His followers to search. Who knows what we will find in life? Who knows what we will find in any one day? Jesus asked us to seek. Yet some people have been programmed to think that if they do not find, they are failures. For them, searching and seeking are anxious experiences. Jesus wanted us to enjoy the journey and the search each day of our lives.

Jesus gave another clue to happiness. He said "knock and it shall be opened..." His method of happiness was good news to those who could hear. But for those whose happiness was limited to fulfilling their expectations, "knock and it shall be opened," was too shallow.

Jesus knew that the secret to happiness was action without fear. We have been taught to be security-conscious and to be private. For many of us, it is difficult to open things that have not yet been opened, to meet people we have never met, to face situations that we have not encountered before. The secret to happiness is the ability to find wonder and surprise everywhere.

From the newness of life that we had as a child when we explored so many things, we have gradually become like hermit crabs. We do move around a little, but there is so much anxiety and fear living in that shell. Gradually, it becomes more difficult to adjust to the light of the world.

When Jesus preached, He gave people simple exercises to do. He promised that the one who asks always receives, the one who searches always finds, and the one who knocks always has the door opened to him. Have you seen it fulfilled during your lifetime?

Life is so unpredictable and we are such free spirits, that each time we ask, seek, or knock it is like new creation up against new creation. We find that in each step God is present. And what we ask for and what we find is God's will unfolding.

MATTHEW 21:22 AND IF YOU HAVE FAITH, EVERYTHING YOU ASK FOR IN PRAYER YOU WILL RECEIVE.

48. ONLY YOU KNOW THE SECRET OF HAPPINESS

Can you remember a day in your life when you were happy from your waking hour until nightfall? You may have been alone, reading or working, or with a friend walking or sharing.

Are you aware of the persons, places and things that give you the most joy? If you have discovered these things and you do them you must be in a constant state of peace.

The keys to happiness are the keys to the kingdom. Sometimes we fail to realize that by finding happiness we have found "The Kingdom" because society has convinced you that the kingdom of God is in the future.

Do you know people who discouraged you from pursuing your own happiness and convinced you that something else was more important? They felt that what was important for them was right for you.

Jesus knew that people hungered for happiness so he emphasized that children had the kingdom already. He encouraged those who listened, to accept the world as a child does. They could be fully themselves as they entered this kingdom He spoke of.

The secret of happiness is found in being alert, having a clear head and an open heart. The kingdom belongs to children and to adult children who appreciate both their strengths and weaknesses as overflowing gifts. You have a font of gifts that pour over you like rain and light, precious thoughts, feelings and actions too numerous to describe.

God's grace is all around. You need not search far and wide. You need not imitate, compare, strain, cling or compete. Neither death nor life can separate you from the Spirit, the grace and the life of God. This is the secret of happiness. You are the secret of happiness. The kingdom belongs to such as you.

ROMANS 8:35 NOTHING CAN COME BETWEEN US AND THE LOVE OF CHRIST, EVEN IF WE ARE TROUBLED OR WORRIED, OR BEING PERSECUTED, OR LACKING FOOD OR CLOTHES, OR BEING THREATENED OR EVEN ATTACKED.

49. FAITH, LIKE LOVE, IS NOT DEMANDING

If we had faith the size of a mustard seed, we would experience the kingdom. For some people, faith means to ingest a set of doctrines and to profess them when necessary. Similarly, conversion traditionally occurs when one adopts a different set of beliefs. Some religious people try to convince others that their doctrines are the best. Depending on the manner that conversions were attempted, the results have varied from tolerance to violence. Throughout history conflicts have been caused by religious pride and righteousness, but primarily through ignorance.

Beliefs that people profess and the ideologies that they defend are often philosophical and secular. Because they are called official pronouncements, they assume extra significance as if religion were more important than human life. This is not spiritual faith, but rather defensiveness based on religious fear. This is not professing your faith, it is aggressive solicitation. It is very offensive.

Can you imagine a world where people left others free? That would be real faith. True faith does not seek to convert.

Faith is a depth of personal seeing. This faith is built on life! It is smaller than a mustard seed, but size doesn't matter. As seeing is non-clinging, so is faith. As you cannot cling to your breathing, you cannot cling to faith. As you cannot capture beauty but must let it flow, as you cannot restart the day, but must let each one pass, so too you cannot hold on to your life. Why would you want to cling when you have God creating new thoughts and feelings and actions?

It might be fun to spend this meditation making a list of the things you believe, that you are giving your life for. Then ask these questions about your beliefs. The moment you think of it, does it give you great joy? Is it so much a part of your life that you are living by this belief? Does the practice of your faith bring life and joy to yourself and others?

I CORINTHIANS 12:8, 9, 11 ONE MAY HAVE THE GIFT OF PREACHING, ANOTHER THE GIFT OF FAITH, ANOTHER THE GIFT OF HEALING... ALL THESE ARE THE WORK OF ONE AND THE SAME SPIRIT, WHO DISTRIBUTES DIFFERENT GIFTS TO DIFFERENT PEOPLE JUST AS HE CHOOSES.

50. LOVING DECISIONS

A decision is your opportunity to add flavor to life! The options you select make you different from the you of yesterday. According to the choices you make each day, you reflect your true feelings and needs. In order to make these healthy choices, you need to realize how free you are. When you are aware you are loved, you immediately feel a profound sense of freedom. Mindful that you are loved and free, you are released from the tentacles of your programming and conditioning.

A decision is truly yours to the extent that you are free in deciding. Fear contaminates the validity of any personal choice. While weighing the alternatives and the consequences is important, being aware that one is unconditionally loved is the greatest help in making confident decisions.

When people are aware, they move with ease through each step of life. They are willing to take risks in the light of their personal preferences. They are sensitive to others, respect others' decisions, and do not insist on their own way. They enjoy the inspirations and surprises that come from within and the unpredictability of creation. People who are aware know the limitations of human nature, especially their own.

DEUTERONOMY 30:20 CHOOSE LIFE, THEN, SO THAT YOU AND YOUR DESCENDANTS MAY LIVE IN THE LOVE OF YAHWEH YOUR GOD.

51. OBSTACLES TO JOY

Sometimes you act as though your heart, mind and body were integrated. On other occasions you notice that there is resistance in your behavior. As you look back on your day, there were times when you were thoroughly involved and rather satisfied. Your attentiveness made time inconsequential. You could have been teaching a class and be so involved with the children that you were unaware of time, or you could have been looking at the sunset.

Notice the things you did during the day that did not bring happiness. As you recognize the particular occasion, see if you can discover the events or the thoughts which interfered with your joy. Little pressures and feelings of obligation can detract from experiencing life fully.

While you are doing something you enjoy, a question may enter your head, "What will other people think of this?" You are then distracted from full participation in the event at hand. To care about others is wonderful. To be interested in their opinions is natural. But to worry about the infinite possibilities of what they might be thinking is a waste of emotional and spiritual energy.

If you feel compelled to do something, expressed by "I have to do it," then you can escape from the burden only by getting "it" over with. The law of "getting it done" is a leech on the spirit of joy; it affects your thinking and behavior.

Heightened emotions also interfere with your freedom and participation. Fear, for example, distracts so much that the emotion itself needs calming before one is able to focus and act normally. Consequently, when emotions are not under control, you are unable to be fully present or fully yourself. Finally, the anticipation of some reward or approval will distract from the joy of this graced present.

Acting with awareness and having your attention focused on things that are real and present are the beginnings of wisdom and will help you grow in joyful self-acceptance.

MATTHEW 6:21 FOR WHERE YOUR TREASURE IS, THERE WILL YOUR HEART BE ALSO.

52. FREEDOM IS SOMETHING WE LIVE

We have a surprising vocation: to be contemplatives in action. We were created to be living centers.

Children are vibrant centers, audibly as well as visibly, observing randomly, demanding selectively. The world as they see it and their reactions are thoroughly unique. Have you noticed how children contemplate and then immediately move into action? It is amazing how children go from one thing to the next with such quickness, with a certainty of what they desire at each moment.

Adults do the same thing when they spend long periods of time intrigued by objects of creation: land, sea and sky, or totally absorbed in the pages of a book. At other times, adults, like children, can do ten things in one minute. Yet the motivation of adults and children varies greatly. Adults will tell you very easily about the things that compel them. They will tell you where their life is filled with obligation and fear. Their description betrays the compulsions of their lives. As frequently as the adult says, "I must, I have to, I should," the child says, "I want." " It is always, "I want to go home; I want to get up; I want to eat; I want to play; I want to go over to my friend's house." Very rarely will you find a child begin a sentence with, "I have to."

Between the adult's seeing and doing lies a set of dictates that interrupts with audacity. It is as though a cloud enters his private thoughts. The cloud says, "What should you be doing now? Are you doing the right thing? Are you living up to the standards that have been impressed upon you? Are you living up to the ideals that you expect of yourself?" When you were a child your self responded directly, now the self responds to an interior program based on "shoulds".

The cloud, this non-self, is hard to escape from because it is not visible; yet nothing can quiet the insatiable "shoulds." An adult so afflicted always walks gingerly, for the slightest stimulus could trigger and broadcast a loud internal screech, "You did the wrong thing."

Self-inflicted punishment occurs as the adult tries to live up to the expectations of the black cloud. When people make a god out of their "black cloud," they are no longer faithful to life but become subject to a conscience-monster and often attempt to preach it to others.

Whom shall we blame for our conscience? No one! Rather than blame, use your energy to find truth and freedom again. One path might be to assess the wasteful anxiety and damage that the "black cloud" inflicts and discover the cloud's destructive character. We have assumed that the concept "what people might think" to be an actual reality. We burdened ourselves further by creating "a god who judges and a cloud that makes me feel guilty." In each situation, I am the victim and the persecutor.

Spend some time on each of these questions that may disperse the illusion of fear. What will I think, what will others think, what will God think, what will my conscience think? First, is there any fear that I could actually reject myself? Second, who are these "other" people that I am intimidated by? Third, "What will god think?" This concept of god is not God any more than a menu is food. It is just another excuse for my not being free. A God who has redeemed me would really not like to hear me blaming Him for my lack of freedom! Fourth, Is "conscience" simply the "black cloud" that I myself have created; or is someone else renting space in my head?

How do we become like little children? How do we accept our responses to life with light-heartedness and with assurance? How can I be true to myself, true to life and never again walk in fear of the clouds of my own creation?

Start with awareness. Watch what happens! Many have travelled this road to freedom. You are not alone; many are sharing it with you. Take it as a daring challenge, a graced opportunity and enjoy the journey.

LUKE 19:40 "I TELL YOU, IF THESE KEEP SILENCE THE STONES WILL CRY OUT."

53. LISTEN TO YOUR HEART

What does it matter if we are successful in the eyes of the world - but unhappy interiorly? Unless we listen to our hearts, we are in constant danger of succumbing to the pressures of power, prestige and praise.

Some people find spectacular events or large gatherings stimulating. Others find happiness in a quiet setting with few people, with simply the drama of nature. Where are you most content?

Have you been pressured not to listen to your heart but to obey some outside authority? It is difficult to manipulate a person when each believes for himself, cherishes his own desires and values his own thoughts.

How do we reclaim a spirit that has been repressed? How do we listen to life and to ourselves? When we were children, loving parents listened to our needs. Then during the process of growing up, some of us were motivated not to trust our own needs or to follow our own will, but to respect and obey the will of authority. Often leadership roles were delegated to those who obeyed and who were able to get other people to obey.

The strange qualifications of leadership were, "Did he conform to standards and could he motivate others to conform to them?" Officials were often those who had received approval from their own superiors. Titles were issued and they commanded respect. And so the system was perpetuated. People in power disguise their selfish plans by claiming that "their will" is best for the country, the organization, the church or the family. They actually claim to know what is right. Religious leaders impressed upon God's people the value of obedience. And so people were ordered to accept the commands of their appointed superiors as though from a much higher authority.

We can easily fall into the same trap. The temptation is to look for certification and acceptance from others. Did Jesus look for positions of authority in institutions? That was not His way.

The way to find happiness and to be spirit-filled is to be aware of our reactions. Notice the lifelessness and the trance-like effects of habits. Be aware of our tendency to judge people in conventional ways. If we find ourselves wishing other people would change, ask, "Why would we want anyone to conform to our standards?" Would we want to conform to someone else's image? We are a new creation today, far different from what we were yesterday. New air surrounds us; new thoughts invite us; new desires recreate us. See, I am making all things new!

How do you repossess your heart and live this new life? One way would be to welcome any challenge that comes or any problem that surfaces with, "Pleased to make your acquaintance; let's have a go at it." Even if you do not express it aloud, you can feel this awareness, like music playing in your soul. In listening to your heart, you will reclaim the secret of happiness.

MARK 2:27 AND HE SAID TO THEM, "THE SABBATH WAS MADE FOR MAN, NOT MAN FOR THE SABBATH;"

54. THE POOR ARE NEAR US

We need to visit the poor. We need to look into their faces and let them see us. We need to listen to their pleas and let them hear our voices. If we do not see the poor, we have not seen life. If we have not touched the poor, we have not touched the truth. To have an appreciation of life, we need to see the victims of greed, competition and power. To have a balanced view of life, we must see those who are damaged by accident and by addiction. To have the whole truth, we need to see those who are devastated by injustice and violence. We must see the Third World that has been created by the First World's accumulations. For millions of human beings, deprivation has been their only heritage.

There are poor people because of the violence of nature and the violence of society. We do not need to figure out which is the poorest of the poor. The ones who are deprived of the world's goods, the ones who are behind bars, or those who must bear arms against God's people are all destitute. The uniforms of the hungry, the prisoners, and the soldiers are different, and their food is very different, but their poverty is very much the same. Lacking freedom, they are living in constant fear of authority, of abuse or of deprivation.

The poor in society are not only the victims of economic greed but also those who live daily in fearful neighborhoods. The poor are those in uniform in the military forces throughout the world, who have been sentenced to obey the arbitrary commands of superiors. They are struggling not just to endure the difficulties of life away from their families but also to survive the commands of authority. Military personnel throughout the world hunger to live in peace in their own homes, sleep in beds that are theirs and live decently with their loved ones.

Jesus had pity on the centurion and on the soldiers even on the night He was condemned. He had compassion for prisoners, and toward the end of His life He Himself became one. He spent much of His time with the poor. He touched them and they improved. He fed them and they cried tears of joy. He spoke with them and their poor hearts danced.

The poor we will always have with us. They are all around. If we look into their eyes, listen to their voices, touch their hands and in turn let them see, hear, and touch us - that is the one thing we can do. They are very much like us; they belong to our family. Like us, each is a child of God. Sometimes we need to be with them, for such is the kingdom of God.

MATTHEW 25:38 - 40 "LORD, WHEN DID WE SEE YOU HUNGRY AND FEED YOU; OR THIRSTY AND GIVE YOU DRINK? WHEN DID WE SEE YOU A STRANGER AND MAKE YOU WELCOME; NAKED AND CLOTHE YOU; SICK OR IN PRISON AND GO TO SEE YOU?' AND THE KING WILL ANSWER, 'I TELL YOU SOLEMNLY, IN SO FAR AS YOU DID THIS TO ONE OF THE LEAST OF THESE BROTHERS OF MINE, YOU DID IT TO ME."

55. WHO ARE YOUR FRIENDS?

There are lifelong friends and there are graced friends. The former are those individuals who have loved you into life and during your life. Graced friends are people who love life and have loved life with you.

To have a community of friends who appreciate each other and who are open to change stimulates the mind and heart. To spend time with people who exchange ideas and who express their affection is a blessing indeed. We need these human signs of grace and freedom in a world where people are submerged in unjust structures and daily pressures.

The focus of business and the decisions of authority are not based on the appreciation of persons. The individual person cannot be the priority of the church or nation and certainly not of the economic community. We ourselves are busy about many things: shopping and housekeeping, entertainment and engagements. People constantly seek success, achievement and security. Institutional values are the same.

Unless you are with people who have an appreciation for life and who truly delight in each other, you become susceptible to lethargic living. Appreciation essentially requires a lovely leap of faith. To believe that God is greater than any creed or dogmatic formulation keeps your capacity for appreciation growing. When you see God as the God of all persons of all history you accept the godliness of each person. When you take the leap of faith at the deepest center of your being and discover that God is nothing but love, then a deep truth surfaces. You are able to accept the enigmatic world that God has made and feel graced with lifelong and newly found friends.

JOHN 17:24 I WANT THOSE YOU HAVE GIVEN ME TO BE WITH ME WHERE I AM, SO THAT THEY MAY ALWAYS SEE THE GLORY YOU HAVE GIVEN ME.

56. UNFULFILLED DESIRES

It seems that I never do the things I really want to do! It seems as though my desires and hopes are so grand that they cannot be satisfied by any series of actions. Often when I see what I have done, it is not what I intended.

Things can be observed and words can describe, but desires cannot be adequately defined. Something affects me and I am left speechless. I often try to give expression to this spirit-filled thing - to no avail.

Understanding the impossibility of putting into effect all that I desire makes it easier to accept myself and my indefinable nature. Accepting that God did not create me to be perfect makes it easier for me to accept my limits, stumblings, and inadequacies. As a consequence, I can look at life and appreciate the beauty. My spirit somehow responds to spirit despite the many obstacles of matter.

As the whole is greater than any of its parts, the spirit is greater than anything we could ever wish for. Each person has the Spirit whether one knows it or not. This is the Good News!

While I am unable to do the things I want to do, I am already doing all that God wants of me; and that is wonderful!

HEBREWS 6:11 OUR ONE DESIRE IS THAT EVERY ONE OF YOU SHOULD GO ON SHOWING THE SAME EARNESTNESS TO THE END.

57. PRAYER WITHOUT END

"Pray always," Jesus said. It was an invitation, understood by the people He spoke to. However, if people are convinced they are not holy, no amount of prayer will convince them. "Always" is not enough.

Time given to prayer has been defined in many ways. Traditionally, it has consisted of recited words. Certain times of each day were set aside for the recitation of carefully selected writings. In certain cultures people were instructed to assume appropriate postures while reciting.

A variety of motivations were given for prayer: some lofty, some threatening. To encourage prayer, sometimes indulgences were offered, sometimes punishment was preached.

Prayer books were approved of and distributed. People were trained to feel relieved when they performed these prayers.

We might ask ourselves, what is the motivation for my prayer? Am I seeking favors from God? Do I feel that God does not give me enough? Am I simply praising God? Am I aware that God has no need of my prayer? Was I taught that God needed my prayers, or that God would only love people if certain prescribed readings were followed? How much is based on obligation, or belief that God's love is contingent upon my prayer? Was I taught that God was capable of increased pleasure and would certainly be happier when I prayed?

When I pray, am I simply doing something I like to do? Do I like to go to a quiet place, to read and think? Do I like to ponder accounts written in the Scriptures and relate them to life's daily mysteries? Is it sufficient motivation that I am doing what I like to do?

The greatest praise that I can give to God is to be the unique person that God has created. What a wholehearted prayer this is!

MATTHEW 6:7, 8 "IN YOUR PRAYERS DO NOT BABBLE; YOUR FATHER KNOWS WHAT YOU NEED BEFORE YOU ASK HIM."

58. THE KINGDOM IS YOUR BIRTHRIGHT

The kingdom of God is shared with you. Those who are unaware that the kingdom of God is already theirs strain and compete, even kill, to win some power, property or position.

Those who are trying to gain the world do not see God is present in every gesture of every day. Instead of rejoicing and being lost in wonder, they feel short-changed, insecure and greedy.

Everyone is selfish to a certain degree, yet each person thinks that her selfishness is justifiable. Nations and churches, like the people that comprise them try to convert as many as possible to accept their particular beliefs. Governments with great wealth seek to gain ever more capital and more reserves. The travesty of secular imperialism and religious expansionism is evident. How difficult it is to be free when one belongs to a power hungry institution! Those in positions of authority within the institutions have the greatest difficulty being free. They find themselves pulled in different directions: the need to submit to authority, the desire to be loyal to their constituents, and the struggle to be true to their own inspirations.

The pressures to conform and submit are great for religious people, for political people, for wealthy people, for all people. Is this what was so challenging about the words, "Unless you lose your life in this world, you shall not find it?" But if it is all God's creation and possession, what are people really struggling for? What are they afraid of losing or striving to gain?

Who taught you to want more, to be dissatisfied with you? Who told you to try to become holier than other people, to be spiritually covetous, or that you were not good enough, holy enough or loved by God enough? You are!

GALATIANS 4:6, 7 GOD HAS SENT THE SPIRIT OF HIS SON INTO OUR HEARTS: THE SPIRIT THAT CRIES, "ABBA, FATHER." YOU ARE NOT A SLAVE ANY MORE; AND IF GOD HAS MADE YOU, HE HAS MADE YOU HIS HEIR.

59. THE GRACE TO BE OPEN

What does it mean to be open and compassionate? If the people who knew you were asked to list your main characteristics would openness be one of them? In a discussion can you hear more than one side of a question and understand that if conditions were different, your view would also be different? Can you admit that your reaction to a situation might have been the same as another person's, given her past conditioning and circumstances?

Think of someone who has very strong opinions. See if you can justify this person's point of view. If you are able to understand that conditioning formed this person, you have the quality of openness.

Since God has created the complex situations that you encounter, there are certain factors to examine if you wish to be open: First, listen to the whole story, listen with interest and you will observe new truths. Second, be willing to change your opinion if the evidence is convincing. Third, notice other approaches, admitting that better ways than yours are possible. The willingness to see that other ways are at least equally acceptable is a tremendous step. It relieves you of the necessity to defend and justify that your way is best. It gives your life greater balance and perspective while you trust your own impressions.

One of the great values of being open is that you can understand more about life. You have the grace to be open to whomever you wish, whenever you like.

LUKE 1:42, 43 SHE GAVE A LOUD CRY AND SAID, "OF ALL WOMEN YOU ARE THE MOST BLESSED, AND BLESSED IS THE FRUIT OF YOUR WOMB. WHY SHOULD I BE HONORED WITH A VISIT FROM THE MOTHER OF MY LORD?"

60. FREEDOM FROM SHYNESS

Shyness is a timid attitude experienced while in the presence of others. Are you aware of certain situations, events or places that reveal your shyness? Some people are noticeably reserved when they are with particular people. Some people telegraph shyness, others make efforts to hide the discomfort.

It might be helpful to look at recent situations to see if shyness still occurs and if so, how often. Recall occasions where people or situations seemed to cause embarrassment. People are often shy if they feel others might evaluate their performance. You might recall participating in specific events where you would have preferred to withdraw. See if you can discover the situation, then the source. Do you notice any pattern in your behavior? Some people are typically shy when they are required to display their talents before an audience, others when the focus is on them - even in having their picture taken. Others are self-conscious sitting face to face, even with their own friends.

Shyness is an emotional reaction that has, by repetition, become a pattern. Shyness originates from a painful experience, a threatening situation or a feeling of being rejected. A shy person by emotional withdrawal attempts to avoid the pressure of being vulnerable.

Shyness can occur as a result of a family or classroom situation where embarrassment is an accepted method of correction. One traumatic event or many repeated experiences can begin the pattern of shyness. If a child feels anxiety in a group or in the presence of an authority, shyness may become a part of his personality.

Why is it valuable to look at the instances when we feel unassertive, reluctant or inadequate? It is important to uncover these sources of fear to expedite our Christ-like pilgrimage.

Certainly God does not want us to be afraid. Jesus wanted no one to be afraid of Him and He would surely never embarrass us. In the book of Isaiah, Yahweh is assuring, "I will never put you to shame." Can you believe this good news? What would enable you to believe that you could walk without fear in all situations?

One of the reasons that it is healthy to discover the source of embarrassment is that shyness is an infliction of pain on oneself! Shyness becomes a masochistic tendency, where I punish myself rather than be in a position to be punished. I reject myself rather than be rejected by others. The infliction is perpetuated and guaranteed: I hit myself and hurt myself.

The exciting good news about this reflection is that once I am aware of my personal performance pattern, I have the first step to freedom. Once I realize that it is "me" doing it to myself, and it is not the present situation, nor this person, nor the size of the crowd that is causing my embarrassment, I can grow. I can get off the painful tack that I have been sitting on.

There is suddenly wonder and clarity. The support pattern that we installed to protect us from pain is no longer needed. A whole new world opens up, since God desires that we would never be embarrassed. With the freedom and courage God has given us, we can then assert our modest selves, our limited selves, our accepted selves, without shyness, without defensiveness, without fear.

There is so much in life to be seen and enjoyed.

ISAIAH 43:4, 5 YOU ARE PRECIOUS IN MY EYES, YOU ARE HONORED AND I LOVE YOU, I GIVE MEN IN EXCHANGE FOR YOU, PEOPLES IN RETURN FOR YOUR LIFE. DO NOT BE AFRAID, FOR I AM WITH YOU...

61. THE WORLD INVADES MY PRAYER

This morning my heartfelt prayer is focused on the daily paper. My spirit goes across the miles as I sense a oneness with my suffering brothers and sisters. I feel united with those who live with injustice and violence. They come before my closed eyes; they fill my mind and heart.

My heart goes south to Central America as I see the military arresting civilians and priests and banning the news media. I pray for the people. I know if I were in their situation I would have deep emotions of fear, anger and frustration. I would beseech God to give me the strength to respond in an appropriate way.

I question why my government supports cruel dictators who are neither of the people, by the people or for the people? I pray for the people who are living in daily danger and constant fear.

In South Africa, a city named Crossroads was visited by the great Bishop Tutu. He walked in the mud of one of the poorest slums in South Africa with Robert Muncey and Coretta King. Walking by the shanties, hearts were transformed as they reached out to the people in their misery. When people really see each other lives are changed.

There is an article in the paper that a Maryknoll missionary has been threatened with expulsion from her Order because she supported a statement on women's rights with many other sisters, priests and lay people.

My wish is that all people could be revered as singularly loved children of God, free to speak their concerns without fear of retribution, and that all political prisoners, hostages and refugees be allowed to return to their homes.

I pray that governments that rule by fear cease to exist. I pray that leaders see firsthand the suffering that oppression causes. I pray that the United States withdraws military and financial support from these cruel regimes, so that the people can choose their own form of government without interference.

I pray that there can be peaceful elections, peaceful political activity and respect for human life.

It would be lovely if all governments and churches were not promoting themselves but were of the people, for the people and by the people.

I pray for government leaders today and for the president who lives in fear of not being re-elected or of slipping in the weapons race.

I pray for the priests who, like Jesus, are in jail and on trial for working among farmers and fishermen. I pray this morning for Sister Rose Trapasso, and other missionaries that they may not be disheartened by the frustrations of injustice.

These conflictual scenes may be miles away and yet they are merely thoughts away. In the safety of our communities, we can bring peace to the world by responding to the invitations that God is sending us.

Jesus gave the example where to start for individuals, for governments, for the various churches. "Love one another as I have loved you."

What shall I pray for this day? Ponder the items in this morning's paper, or the "National Catholic Reporter" or "America" magazine.

I TIMOTHY 6:16 THE KING OF KINGS AND THE LORD OF LORDS, WHO ALONE IS IMMORTAL, WHOSE HOME IS IN INACCESSIBLE LIGHT, WHOM NO MAN HAS SEEN AND NO MAN IS ABLE TO SEE: TO HIM BE HONOR AND EVERLASTING POWER. AMEN.

62. GOD LOVES US WITHOUT EFFORT

Most people try to shape their behavior as if they were both the craftsman and the clay. Who told you that you were two? Where did you get the idea that you could improve on what God created? How did you learn to have a demanding dictator self and a subservient self within you?

Can you remember the last time you made an effort to do something? It was as though there were two persons: one person functioning and another person exhorting. Is it possible to manipulate yourself, to make a slave of yourself so that there is a master and a servant? Some people do this and they justify the division by saying, "My master makes demands on me, but then he rewards me when I conform." Does that ever happen to you? Do you find some interior authority urging you to accomplish more, an imaginary authority that gives and withholds permissions and rewards?

The people who experience two voices do not perceive this present individual as he is, but find themselves judging what the other's behavior ought to be. Are not the ideals we pray for better than the reality that exists? Notice the theme of their prayers is for God to change the world according to their own image. They are innocently asking God to do more, as if God has not done enough. The obvious implication is that God could improve.

The subtlety of this kind of prayer is that we are hoping to manipulate God. Life is a struggle with pain and sorrow, failures and rejections with death incorporated into the plan. There is a great desire to want life to be perfect and for all things to be in harmony. While this yearning is beautiful, the ability to see and to accept the world with all of its diversity is sublime.

There is an impatience in us that has been passed on from generation to generation. We would like our ideals to become real. Yet the desire to want it now is the cause of our restlessness.

God welcomes you each day as you are. God accepts the injustice of the world, its failures, rejections and sufferings, without judging, condemning, or convicting the world. God understands the world's frustrations and our impossible ideals. How marvelous to believe that we will always be God's loved creatures until the end of time! We are redeemed in God's love. What a consoling response to our humble efforts and hopes!

2 CORINTHIANS 5:19 GOD IN CHRIST WAS RECONCILING THE WORLD TO HIMSELF, NOT HOLDING MEN'S FAULTS AGAINST THEM, AND HE HAS ENTRUSTED TO US THE NEWS THAT THEY ARE RECONCILED.

A Rose in December: Maura Clarke, MM

A Rose in December: Jean Donovan

63. DISCOVERING YOUR FREEDOM

Has anyone ever asked you how you became free? What a compliment!

I think every person feels that he is somewhat unique, but when someone uses the adjective "free", it is a gift and a challenge. For God did not create us to be slaves, fearful, or one of the bunch, but to be free. Only a free person is able to love.

When Jesus walked the earth, He loved to announce freedom to people. Jesus spent his time with people who thought that He was free and He found freedom in the people with whom He spent His time. As He announced this good news, many could not believe it. Many must have laughed openly when Jesus announced this unrealistic good news. Who else had ever told them that their origin and destiny was love, and that in the eyes of God they were innocent? Most of them had curious and sincere questions, "Where did He come from? Where did He get such wisdom? How does He know me?"

Has anyone ever asked you, "How did you become free?" Until someone else recognizes it in you, you are probably not acting freely or you are not spending enough time with free people. Those who recognize your freedom have a special gift themselves and they are invaluable to you.

When do you experience freedom? The discovery begins with an unusual sensation. It feels dramatic, relaxing and refreshing at the same time. There is a sense of release as though you stopped carrying fifty pounds of baggage. There is a sense of surprise as though you were lost, and suddenly found the way.

Why are you not always free? Observe four types of anxiety: in people who are programmed, in those who live in fear, in those who are trying to become better and in those who are pressured to change. Observe the things that people are afraid of, indebted to, striving for, and you will discover the invisible obstacles to freedom.

When you do what you really want you might feel unworthy, because you were taught exceptionally well how to deny yourself, how to upset yourself, even how to harm yourself.

Sometimes you make a decision and you are certain that it is not really yours. You know it immediately! You are not really following your deepest desires. Whose decision is it? What a mystery!

You can observe very clear signs of true freedom from children. If you want to begin the process spend some quality time (awareness time, not responsible time) with little ones.

You have the opportunity to grow in freedom whenever you wish. When you experience freedom in your decisions, you will be smiling regularly. Freedom is your nature and grace.

If you have time to hear a lovely story, ask your friend, "How did you become free?"

GALATIANS 5:1 WHEN CHRIST FREED US, HE MEANT US TO REMAIN FREE. STAND FIRM, THEREFORE, AND DO NOT SUBMIT AGAIN TO THE YOKE OF SLAVERY.

The Rose of Guatemala: Sr. Barbara Ford, SC

64. FOSTERING UNCONDITIONAL ACCEPTANCE

If we believe that God created us, then God desired us and gave us life. God wanted us to be visible, so we were made incarnate. God wanted us to relate to other creatures so we were given the ability and desire to respond to each other.

While all of God's creatures are unique, their perceptions and responses to each other and to the Creator are also unique. Yet certain natural laws are discoverable in the observation of these creatures.

For a law to be good it must serve the common good. Since laws are determined by the conditioning and orientation of the committee in power, they can easily suppress rather than enhance the good of people.

While some countries "legally" supported slavery, assisted repressive dictatorships and refused to provide sanctuary for frightened individuals, other nations fortunately implemented laws that provided refuge for people who were fleeing poverty, hunger, war and religious oppression. When the poor and powerless were labeled "enemies of the state" Churches frequently rescued them. Some families jeopardized their own lives by granting shelter to these innocent victims of violence.

Do not be surprised if you meet very few people who accept all people as brothers and sisters in the family of God. Do not be shocked when you discover your own veneer of cultural conditioning. You have been deeply conditioned to view people in categories. You have been instructed to separate, label and, ever so subtly, to judge.

Is there any answer to this political, religious and economic disease of non-seeing that has reached epidemic proportions? What helped Jesus? On the many occasions when Jesus did not agree with the literal views of the chief priests, civil leaders or His own disciples He prayed, "As the Father and I are one, so you and I are one."

When I find the president of one country unwilling to dialogue or break bread with the president of another country, or worse, calling an air strike on his family, mining a Central American country's only harbor or effecting the overthrow of a South American country's elected president, it helps me not to condemn angrily if I say, "President, you and I are one."

When I hear a religious leader saying that separated brothers and sisters are not welcome at the banquet table and that he does not want his ministers to break bread with these brothers and sisters, I find it helpful and humbling to say, "Father, you and I are one."

It might be helpful too, when using this prayer, if you refer to these powerful officials by their first names. It helps to verbalize that these persons, although having exalted titles, are as human as the least of us.

When someone makes a judgment that you do not share, and you wonder how this person could possibly think the way he does, listen to yourself say, "You and I are one."

JOHN 3:32, 35 HE WHO COMES FROM HEAVEN BEARS WITNESS TO THE THINGS HE HAS SEEN AND HEARD. HE WHOM GOD HAS SENT SPEAKS GOD'S OWN WORDS: GOD GIVES HIM THE SPIRIT WITHOUT RESERVE. THE FATHER LOVES THE SON AND HAS ENTRUSTED EVERYTHING TO HIM.

65. BEING HAPPY WITH
YOUR DECISIONS

We make thousands of choices every day. There is grace and excitement as this wonderful coordinated machine of spiritual neurons goes into action. When a little child chooses his cereal for breakfast, pours on the sugar and milk, and watches the flakes rise over the bowl onto the table, something strange inside of him tells him to stop pouring the milk. As he dabs his fingers in the spilled milk, he eats the flakes from the table. How many decisions did he make?

Where to sit, what to eat, when to go, how to act are little decisions everyone makes from childhood through adulthood, minute by precious minute. There is a pattern and a person at the center of each choice. It is you; or is it?

I asked a child the other day, when she had awakened from her nap, if she had been sleeping. She laughed at me and shook her head, "No." We both laughed expressing our happiness as loud as possible.

The important choices are as easy as the small ones when the goal is clear and the decision maker is at peace. If the goal is not clear then time for reflection is necessary. If the person is not at peace, he needs time to become restful and confident.

One purpose of meditation is to discover with great clarity what your desire is. It is important that the person experiences the difference between the integrity of being satisfied with oneself from the security of measuring up to someone else's standards. Integrity is who you are and something that you live. Measuring up is a tentative, uneasy type of joy that depends on outside forces and others' approval. If you live according to someone else's standards you may become successful but you will never be happy.

Many organizations, military and otherwise, want prospective candidates to join their formation program and obey orders. How many people have fallen into the trap of measuring up to authority's expectations? Could any program form you better than God and loving parents?

Here are certain helps that will bring clarity to decision making.

First, picture yourself twenty years from now. Picture your age, your environment and then look back to today from that point of view. See which decision you would like to have made. This temporal perspective provides healthy detachment so that you know what you desire from a new perspective.

Second, picture your dearest friend in the precise situation and circumstances that you are in. Realizing how much you care for this friend, reflect with his or her best interest in mind. What advice comes to mind? This objectivity and intimacy can provide interesting insights.

Third, picture yourself walking with Jesus who accepts you as His dearest friend. You discover without a shadow of a doubt that He has loved you during every minute of your life. You feel very free because you know that no matter which choice you made His love is the same. If you were to talk to Him about a particular choice you had made, which would it be?

All God cares about is your happiness.

JEREMIAH 31:33, 34 DEEP WITHIN THEM I WILL PLANT MY LAW, WRITING IT ON THEIR HEARTS. THEN I WILL BE THEIR GOD AND THEY SHALL BE MY PEOPLE. THERE WILL BE NO FURTHER NEED FOR NEIGHBOR TO TRY TO TEACH NEIGHBOR, OR FOR BROTHER TO SAY TO BROTHER, "LEARN TO KNOW YAHWEH!" NO, THEY WILL ALL KNOW ME, THE LEAST NO LESS THAN THE GREATEST - IT IS YAHWEH WHO SPEAKS - SINCE I WILL FORGIVE THEIR INIQUITY AND NEVER CALL THEIR SIN TO MIND.

66. FULLY PRESENT: FULLY ALIVE

Hopefully, during most of your life, you are doing what you choose with the people you prefer, at the places and times you select. Hopefully, it is a rare occurrence that you are doing something you do not enjoy, in a place that is not satisfying, with people who are not nourishing. If the latter situation occurs and you find yourself unhappy, how quickly do you resolve this situation so that it will not be repeated? If there is frequent repetition of discomfort, like the feeling of being cornered, you will need some outside help.

Be aware of the times during the day when you are not truly involved because you are not fully present. Sometimes you can be so accustomed to having a low degree of happiness, so habituated to mistrusting your will and choosing what is really not your own desire, that you develop a tolerance for passivity. This is the price you pay when you do not assert your will.

A majority of people have been programmed to believe that the will of authority is not selfish and is actually superior to their own will and that their own desires are selfish! Often they are not responding with their own unique charism because they were taught to subjugate their desires.

It is difficult to be fully alive when you do not even want to be present. Like a child who dislikes being confined and wrestles free, there are clear signals when you do not wish to be in a certain place. How can you be fully yourself when you do not want to be where you are? When you feel confined, you move hopefully to break free. Can you remember the last time you did something for which you had little enthusiasm or went somewhere that you did not really want to go? The true self was not where the physical body appeared.

When you examine your life, realize that on certain occasions you were afraid to follow your heart. Discover this fear that prevents you from listening to your spirit. What past messages do you submit to? It is important to discover the programming that imprisons you.

How do you regain control of your life so that you trust and follow your inspirations? Believing that God loves and accepts you eternally, helps. Why would you believe in anything less than a loving God?

When you do not take time to listen to your desires, your behavior loses its flavor and becomes dull. When you are dissatisfied with a particular choice, see if the decision was not yours. Live, personal decisions are needed for present events.

Aren't you amazed that even people whom you care about and who care about you influence your behavior? Somehow the need for their approval can become stronger than your love for them. Where does that spring from?

When fear diminishes, love becomes the predominant motivation. You will be doing what your heart wants to do, sharing what you want to share, going where you wish to go.

What a joy it is to walk in the light; sometimes it is starlight, sometimes moonlight, sometimes sunlight, but always and everywhere there is God's light.

JOHN 16:23, 24 I TELL YOU MOST SOLEMNLY, ANYTHING YOU ASK FOR FROM THE FATHER HE WILL GRANT IN MY NAME. UNTIL NOW YOU HAVE NOT ASKED FOR ANYTHING IN MY NAME. ASK AND YOU WILL RECEIVE, SO YOUR JOY WILL BE COMPLETE.

67. DECISIONS AND DISCERNMENT

When people make authentic decisions, certain criteria are present: sufficient knowledge of the facts, a fair estimate of the consequences and some awareness of their emotional response.

The issue may be vocation, occupation, relating or locating. Whether a decision is healthy or destructive, right or wrong depends on the one judging.

Some people make apparently difficult choices quite easily. They seem to know how they feel, what their choices will entail, and what will bring them happiness. They seem to be well aware of the degree of sacrifice and commitment required. They seem to act with tranquillity.

Sometimes the facts are not available or the implications are not clear. Then there is the need to withdraw, to choose a process that will bring clarity and understanding. Will I work in the missions or at home? Will I spend most of my time in an urban or rural area? Will I labor with my hands or with my words? Will my staple be rice or potatoes?

Some basic prerequisites for significant discernment include the following. First is the realization of God's loving indifference. Meditate on the thought that whatever choice you make, it does not make any difference to God, to the church or society. Recall that God's love for you is not dependent on your choices. This awareness helps you realize that it really does not matter, the pressure is removed. It seems so easy when it is believed. Can you imagine the Lord saying to you, "Will it be rice or potatoes? I love you. My love is everlasting, infinite and unconditional."

Second is a sense of openness, a willingness to consider all the possibilities, by which you are able to find options you would not have dreamed of.

A third requirement is that you know what you like, what you want, when something tastes good and when someone is good for you.

A fourth prerequisite is assertiveness, the courage to seek for the things you want and ask for the things you need. Assertiveness must be practiced especially if you consider yourself to be a conformist or a follower.

A fifth is emotional peace. There needs to be calm before, during and after this decision process.

Regardless of your inclination, preference or decision, God will fully support you. There are no hidden conditions on God's love; there is no hidden meaning to God's will. And the decision is only significant because you are significant. All your choices are within God's domain and somehow God's responsibility. Remember everything belongs to God, including you.

While the details will always be complex, and the times and places will vary greatly, it is no big deal. As you go through life, which way shall you go? Big decision? Not really! Not to God! You will traverse the world and you will live your life with millions of decisions. What does it matter? You will always be you and you will always have the Lord's affection. You are God's will!

EPHESIANS 1:4, 5 BEFORE THE WORLD WAS MADE, HE CHOSE US IN CHRIST, TO BE HOLY AND SPOTLESS, AND TO LIVE THROUGH LOVE IN HIS PRESENCE, DETERMINING THAT WE SHOULD BECOME HIS ADOPTED SONS.

68. THE IMPORTANCE OF CHOOSING

If you could pick one thing that would differentiate one human being from another, would it be the ability to reason, the freedom to make choices or the capacity to love?

Healthy choosing requires a present awareness of life and a synthesis of past experiences. The choices you make are the choices that make you. What makes you new today are choices that differ essentially from yesterday's; the energy, reflection and joy vary greatly. Your choosing freely makes you uniquely human.

What shall you do today, with whom, where, for how long? How shall you act today: quietly, expressively, dynamically, productively?

One of the common obstacles to freedom is habit. While repetition makes a thing easier to do, it can make performing in a creative way difficult. Habits are best when they free us to do more exciting and innovative things.

Can you feel the energy in each decision? Feelings are so unique that no labels can describe them. It is interesting that words, our customary way of referring to any experience, limit the full realization of the experience. It would be great if we could call each event by a totally different name. Our joy of three days ago, the joyful experience we had yesterday, and the one we are having right now are all different. If we have a fresh way of looking at things, then our joy will be fresh, as with a child who goes from one joy to the next.

One of the incomparable delights of being human is the experience of choosing. Our joy increases dramatically when this precious gift is used with awareness. The freedom to choose is the most spiritual of gifts.

Authority and tradition had forced people to be fearful of the law and of the officials of the law. Jesus came to bring down the mighty from their thrones and to lift up the lowly. Jesus came into the world to announce redemption, so that people would no longer be slaves to the law. Jesus came to bring life and "The Good News" to those under the law, to those making the law, and to those who were poor mercenaries of the law.

It might be worthwhile to examine which officials and which laws present obstacles to your freedom. God never intended you to be fearful of anyone or anything. Christ freed you from the fear of death and from the fear of life. This fearlessness is what makes you fully human. Fearless choices make you Christ-like, while this ability to love makes you God-like.

What do you think would set you free so that your heart would dance, so that your joy would be ongoing and complete? Can you specify the particular freedom that would take away all fear from your life?

1 JOHN 3:1, 2 THINK OF THE LOVE THAT THE FATHER HAS LAVISHED ON US, BY LETTING US BE CALLED GOD'S CHILDREN; AND THAT IS WHAT WE ARE. MY DEAR PEOPLE, WE ARE ALREADY THE CHILDREN OF GOD BUT WHAT WE ARE TO BE IN THE FUTURE HAS NOT YET BEEN REVEALED; ALL WE KNOW IS, THAT WHEN IT IS REVEALED WE SHALL BE LIKE HIM BECAUSE WE SHALL SEE HIM AS HE REALLY IS.

69. WE ARE ALL ONE

Did you ever hear a politician say, "We are the biggest, the best, the richest and the strongest country in the world?" Can you recall your initial reaction to someone's claim that "something" was the best in the world? Can you recall if you had a feeling of pride that somehow your nation had the wealthiest resources or the most destructive weapons? Was your first reaction one of disgust? Of what good is it to gain the whole world?

When you attended a sporting event and you heard the fanatics chanting, "We're number one!" did you have a feeling of pride, or did you experience divisiveness in this singsong notion?

Recall the charming possessiveness of a child, "My bicycle is better than yours. My daddy is better than your daddy. How simplistic and childish!

Did you ever meet an evangelist, priest, rabbi or preacher who exclaimed that his alone was the "one true church"? How simplistic! Did you feel proud, or did you hear it as a typically righteous phrase preached in most religious assemblies?

When adults parrot that same superiority and insecurity by saying, "My descendants and my traditions are better than yours," the best description for the statement as well as the speakers is ridiculous. If they are serious, they are condemning other people to be second class. Maybe they are unwittingly degrading themselves, knowing that the last shall be first! It is telling other people, "God is not present and praised and blest in your congregation as He is in mine." When religious people claim to possess the truth, it is primarily a sign of ignorance and insecurity. How does such childish pride and insecurity infiltrate the message that "God is love"?

Aware people understand that all are God's children. Jesus' message continuously encouraged His disciples not to brag, but to serve, and to look for the last place rather than the first.

Anyone who wants to be considered better than his neighbor has been conditioned, like people who have eyes but cannot see, who have ears but do not hear, who have hearts with little compassion.

When people claim they belong to the one true church, or that they are number one, it helps to imagine them as children exclaiming, "My daddy is better than your daddy." We can smile because they are talking about the same Father. There is only one daddy, there is only one Father and one God. In their ignorance, they do not realize that their God is our God, that the one who created and redeemed them is the God of Abraham, and the God of Jesus and the God of all people of all time. God has promised through many prophets that all will be one. All are one already. There is no need to compare, compete, or convert. In time and beyond time all will know God and enjoy God's love forever.

We can smile with understanding. The world has enough judgment; it has enough militarism and competition. Comparisons, as to who is the best and the strongest, only lead to violence. If churches or nations must compete, let them show forth their power to be compassionate, to grant sanctuary, to protest political torture. Let them act courageously for human rights.

We must smile because we know that God's people are loved, especially the poor and the ignorant and even those who chant, "We're number one."

LUKE 22:26, 27 THE GREATEST AMONG YOU MUST BEHAVE AS IF HE WERE THE YOUNGEST, THE LEADER AS IF HE WERE THE ONE WHO SERVES. FOR WHO IS THE GREATER: THE ONE AT TABLE OR THE ONE WHO SERVES? THE ONE AT TABLE, SURELY. YET HERE AM I AMONG YOU AS ONE WHO SERVES!

70. ARE YOU SATISFIED WITH YOURSELF?

Healthy children do not want to become adults. In an atmosphere of love they are satisfied just as they are. When they are taken to the zoo, they enjoy the animals, the walk, the ride, the sights, and the food. They might make a funny face like the monkey, but they do not want to become a monkey. No, they are satisfied being who they are.

When we kick a ball to a little child and he kicks it back, he is not thinking of becoming a professional. He likes to play, mimic and perform an assortment of movements. When he is surrounded by love, he does not want to become anything else in the world. The love he is experiencing is totally satisfying.

What makes a child want to become something other? Who or what convinces a child to think that she could be better than she is? Can we help children to trust their feelings and accept their responses to life?

It was so interesting when Jesus said, "Unless you become like little children..."He implied that unless you accept who you are you are going to miss the Kingdom. What a chore, to become who you are and to enjoy who you become!

Look at your desires. Write them and discover whether or not they are really yours. If they are appetites that society has taught you, then they are not yours. Once you trace their alien nature, they will have no power over you. The source of unhappiness occurs by attempting to gratify someone else's desires at the expense of your own! Once you observe this, you will laugh.

As you examine the desires of just one day, how many are already being satisfied? If you realized how many desires have been fulfilled in one day, you would be buoyant!

Look at a child today. As she reaches out to you with her eyes, her steps, and her hands, it is easy to see the hundreds of times in every hour that her little desires are being satisfied. It is so easy to see the way to happiness. A healthy child wants to remain a child, to be herself, completely satisfied with who she is.

This is the message. Be who you are. You are a little being who has many desires. You, who are an adult child of God, have desires, hopes and numerous opportunities. Your body and mind have desires which need expression. If you could respond to your true desires as purely as a child, you would find daily happiness.

What a great thrill it is to know that today is your day to enjoy the kingdom! In finding happiness for yourself you will be radiant and you will bring light to others.

2 THESSALONIANS 2:14 GOD CHOSE YOU FROM THE BEGINNING TO BE SAVED BY THE SANCTIFYING SPIRIT AND BY FAITH IN THE TRUTH. THROUGH THE GOOD NEWS THAT WE BROUGHT HE CALLED YOU TO THIS SO THAT YOU SHOULD SHARE THE GLORY OF OUR LORD JESUS CHRIST.

71. SEE FOR YOURSELF

What will people think? This simple question is a powerful motive for avoiding personal decisions. Yet this inquisitive expression directs the lives of many people. It is legitimate to wonder what people think, because they do! But it is ludicrous, because what others think is immeasurable.

To the degree that "What will people think" influences your behavior, no personal motives are possible. Were you taught to doubt your interior stirrings? Why did you mistrust your unique abilities? How did your fresh awareness of life change to whimpering apprehension?

You cannot act honestly when you are motivated by fear. When you can hear a voice saying, "What will people think" it is a red flag to come back to meditation and to bring any decision back to the drawing board.

What will people think? What will the whole world from Nairobi to Irkutsk think? What will those who have died think? Since it is a common question, the fact that it is impersonal and suspicious is overlooked. "What will people think?" Whenever you are guided by that expression, you are distracted by fears induced by past programs.

Put any fear under the microscope of awareness; it would be like analyzing darkness with bright light. Once you confront fear with love and freedom, the fear disappears. In a movie theatre, if you were to move from your chair, walk up and touch the screen, the images would lose their effect. If you put your hand over the lens of the projector the pictures actually disappear. When you step up and see for yourself, previous illusions give way to present reality.

Maybe your conditioning and the power of society's approval have had too much influence on you. You are surrounded by people who are living by standards that others have set. It is a seductive milieu. Have you grown so accustomed to approval, and to the accompanying anxiety, that peace and simplicity are less attractive than they sound? "What will people think?" Could that statement ever again delay you from growing in love? Will you ever let it influence your life again? Can you imagine going through life unencumbered?

Can you plant seeds of trust once again? The only temptation you will face is "What will people think?"

EPHESIANS 3:17 - 19 PLANTED IN LOVE AND BUILT ON LOVE, YOU WILL WITH ALL THE SAINTS HAVE STRENGTH TO GRASP THE BREADTH AND THE LENGTH, THE HEIGHT AND THE DEPTH; UNTIL, KNOWING THE LOVE OF CHRIST, WHICH IS BEYOND ALL KNOWLEDGE, YOU ARE FILLED WITH THE UTTER FULLNESS OF GOD.

Martyr of El Salvador: Bishop Oscar Romero

72. BELIEVE WHAT YOU LIKE

When Jesus realized how conditioned his disciples and the crowds were, He would delight in waking them up. I find Jesus smiling through so many of the Gospel stories. They are precious stories to reflect on.

When I started giving retreats, I memorized the Annotations of the Spiritual Exercises of St. Ignatius and knew them by number. After a while, I emphasized scripture passages on retreat. I knew them by chapter and verse too. If someone presented a theme to me, I would give them a few selections from the Old or New Testament. Recently, I find myself more content with the verses and chapters found in life, and the mysteries faced every day. Now Ignatian and Biblical verses serve as confirming references and helpful footnotes.

Remember when the disciples were anxious about who would be "first" in the kingdom? They did not understand that it was here and now and all around, that there was no such thing as "first", except figuratively, spatially or temporally. First was not a reality.

On one occasion, James and John brought their mother along. They assured her that she would be in first place if they could secure the places next to Jesus. Jesus reading their hearts said, "You are certainly welcome to share my work and drink my cup, but that reward is not mine to give!" They must have gulped at that response.

Jesus responded to life so compassionately. So much of Jesus' humanity is revealed in the scriptures. How daring were the evangelists to relate that Jesus left his parents for three days, that He got angry in the temple and that He told His disciples that He was scandalized by them! When He was told His family was waiting outside for Him, how courageous the gospel writers were to quote Jesus, "Everyone who does the will of God is My father, mother, brother and sister!" Jesus also shocked the religious leaders saying if they wished to have a place with him then they must wash each other's feet, sell their possessions and be identified as poor! Oh, this hurt!

This message woke people up to a whole new way of looking at life; the message still must be announced. Wake up spirituality is as important today as it was in the time of Jesus.

The poor and the underprivileged believed they were neglected by nature, society and apparently by God. To be healthy, clothed and fed is certainly a natural blessing but to be without life's basic necessities does not mean one is neglected by God. Jesus' message was relief for the poor, the slaves, women and the sick. But it was a threatening statement to anyone of the establishment coveting wealth and power.

A woman who felt burdened because she had many talents felt that God was asking too much of her. Every time she discovered a new gift, she felt an unbearable burden of obligation! Were you ever worried that God would judge you harshly because you had been given so much? How easily people become scrupulous and lose their happiness!

Did you ever strive to be perfect in order to be rewarded by god? What a concept of God! What poor theology! Did you ever fear the punishment of God? You were on an emotional, co-dependent roller coaster whenever you accepted authority without question.

What makes a person wake up? The ones who have difficulty waking up are those who feel responsible and who are assigned to program others. It is difficult to give up a career of directing others when fear and approval have been the prime motivation. Let us not be afraid to confront our conditioning and realize how we have been influenced. Let us have the grace to see the innocence and the fear beneath the facade of power. Let us see for ourselves, listen with our hearts and in so doing believe the Good News.

JOHN 5:44 HOW CAN YOU BELIEVE, SINCE YOU LOOK TO ONE ANOTHER FOR APPROVAL?

73. PEACEFUL DECISIONS

Have you noticed how easy it is for you to make decisions on some occasions and on others it seems impossible? To decide means to sift through and cut away other options. Sometimes we are confronted with too many variables. At other times we discover that we were not fully present when we were weighing the options. The timing can be delayed when there is not sufficient information or clarity to make a definitive choice.

Two elements that make a decision personally yours are: 1) having no pressure from outside to disturb your interior peace, and 2) an acceptance of being loved. Peace provides an atmosphere for listening, feeling and observing for yourself. Love enables you to fully appreciate your interior stirring without fear of consequences.

Sometimes when we are alone and peaceful, we are able to see things clearly and to be aware of our inmost desires. When we are confident, we are drawn to respond lovingly and decisions seem to come quite easily. But it is not the quiet place which is important as much as one's interior peace.

It is easy to neglect the time we need for our deepest thoughts. Often we get lost in business and entertainment and we do not attend to the people and works that nourish us most.

Let personal decisions flow from loving selves and uncluttered hearts. These intimate moments are precious.

JOHN 17:13, 23 WHILE STILL IN THE WORLD I SAY THESE THINGS TO SHARE MY JOY WITH THEM TO THE FULL. WITH ME IN THEM AND YOU IN ME, MAY THEY BE SO COMPLETELY ONE THAT THE WORLD WILL REALIZE THAT IT WAS YOU WHO SENT ME AND THAT I HAVE LOVED THEM AS MUCH AS YOU LOVED ME.

74. BREATHING FREELY

People in power are understandably terrified of democracy, of one vote for each person, of everyone counting in life. What would happen if the poor had an equal voice, or if every member of a corporation had an equal vote, or if women had equal rights in every religion: Christian, Muslim, Jew, Mormon?

The reason it is so difficult for women to become organized, is the same reason that it took so many centuries for laborers to have any rights while confronting the inheritors of land, or for slaves to obtain a human place in society.

True power resides in God's people. In the Philippines, women actually stood up to the tanks of Marcos. In Nicaragua the people overthrew the dictator Somoza, only to be beaten down by weapons from El Norte and the CIA. People are temporarily overwhelmed by the power of the military; yet people have a spirit that cannot be quelled. While wealth and weapons seem superior, the will of God's people endures. God's grace and strength reside in the hearts of every person regardless of color, and in every woman regardless of the restrictions of tradition.

As prison bars do not quench a poet's spirit, and armies cannot kill the desire for freedom, police states offer only temporary repression. The hearts of God's people are restless. Every human heart knows what peace is, what love is, and what freedom is. Imperialists and dictators with their armies and weapons will pass away. Voices will be heard and freedom will ring just as the Iron Curtain was torn down almost single-handedly, yet unknowingly, by Sakarov and Gorbachev. Each woman in the church has her own voice crying for freedom. That voice will be heard as surely as Christ's redemption was meant for all. We shall hear it during our lifetime. For while God is everywhere, God is especially present with people who hunger for freedom and peace and with those who work with the poor.

And every voice will be heard and every vote will be counted. Cory's Aquino's voice was heard against political odds. Bishop Tutu's voice was heard against racial odds. People like Teresa Kane will be heard against religious odds.

WISDOM 3:1, 8, 9 THE SOULS OF THE VIRTUOUS ARE IN THE HANDS OF GOD. WHEN THE TIME COMES FOR HIS

*VISITATION THEY WILL SHINE OUT. THEY WILL UNDER-
STAND THE TRUTH AND WILL LIVE WITH HIM IN LOVE;
FOR GRACE AND MERCY AWAIT THOSE HE HAS CHOSEN.*

Celina Maricet Ramos
27 February 1973 -16 November 1989

Elba Julia Ramos
5 March 1947 - 16 November 1989

75. HOW CAN PEOPLE KILL?

How can a boy don a uniform, leave his family and country, trespass on another's land and kill the individuals who reside there? How is it possible for human beings, who are made in the image of God, who are created to love and be loved, join a company, bear weapons and kill other children of God?

What factors could justify the maiming of others? If jobs were scarce, would the offer of money do it? If the government offered honors, praise and financial security, could an intelligent, sensitive human being submit to this bribe? Given this inducement, a man must surrender his will, risk his life and destroy people and property. Why would anyone surrender his freedom and make a career of destroying God's creatures?

Maybe those who are susceptible do not believe in their own goodness or that all people are God's children. Maybe they were never taught about the innocence of their neighbor, or that God created all men and women good.

Maybe the required motivation to sacrifice one's life and to destroy other lives is having a fanatical belief in evil, though another plausible excuse is having a severe emotional disorder. People can be destructive when they are overwhelmed with fear, or suffering themselves from ignorance or insanity. Fear is a terrifying emotional illness that impedes normal human reactions; ignorance is the inability to know what one is doing, and insanity is a severe deterioration of the mental processes.

Indoctrination, whether political or religious, causes people to lose their true identity, for it is the process by which a person is induced with someone else's system of beliefs. While it is presented in an attractive, emotional and logical fashion, the person is then coerced to ingest it. Indoctrination graphically portrays evil, condemns certain individuals as responsible for it and stirs up hatred for these perpetrators. When this mental drug is imbibed, a violent rage ensues that condemns anyone associated with these alien notions. The slightest stimulus can unleash the effects of the original indoctrination.

Primary candidates for indoctrination are idealists, deprived individuals and inexperienced youths. Once innocent human beings are brought into the clutches of people who train them to hate the world, to hate their neighbors, to see evil where authorities want them to see evil, it is as easy to train them as it is to bribe a child. With an atmosphere of fear and frenzy, hatred and coercion, the youths lose their integrity, their beauty and their lovely spirit.

And so those who fight and maim and go to war are not simply motivated by financial security nor are they sufficiently rewarded by medals and promotions. These poor people working for violent governments throughout the world are equally fearful and victimized themselves.

God have mercy on the many victims, frequently young men like themselves whom they destroy, ironically, in the name of honor and country and God.

JOHN 15:18, 19 "IF THE WORLD HATES YOU, REMEMBER THAT IT HATED ME BEFORE YOU. IF YOU BELONGED TO THE WORLD, THE WORLD WOULD LOVE YOU AS ITS OWN; BUT BECAUSE YOU DO NOT BELONG TO THE WORLD, BECAUSE MY CHOICE WITHDREW YOU FROM THE WORLD, THEREFORE THE WORLD HATES YOU."

76. SURVIVAL AND THE CROSS

The First Degree of Humility from the Spiritual Exercises of St. Ignatius challenges God's people to avoid violence against mankind at all costs. It indicates that a person is willing to give his own life and livelihood rather than do anything to cause the injury of another.

This First Degree is extremely threatening for people in military service, in national security positions and in arms production. A society swept up in an "economic" weapons race destroys innocent people worldwide. Millions of people of all faiths produce weapons of mass destruction. Some are paid and some are conscripted in "service" organizations. Others called "intelligence" agents use torture to exact information. There are great numbers of people who work for companies that make bombs, cattle prods and anti-personnel mines. These demoralized and victimized people work in factories achieving their personal goals by producing weapons of destruction.

Others from offices in Washington trade weapons with other countries. The international cancer spreads as they get paid from overt and covert agencies whose existence is dependent on the proliferation of weapons. They are working with "legitimate" corporations as they manufacture terror and export torment. Motivated by high salaries and prestige, they become victims of the system.

During Ignatius' army career he witnessed the illusions of glory and the violence perpetrated in the name of honor, country and obedience. Privileges, status and wealth were granted for chivalry, but beneath the glorious labels and rewards, there was death and suffering.

If leaders could see the victims of war, they would not force young men to kill God's children. If government leaders could see the victims of war, what is happening to civilians by land mines, and if they could really see the connection between Star Wars, "Defense" budgets and the resultant worldwide suffering, I am sure they would cease the carnage.

We are all responsible: the soldiers carrying weapons, the men on large destructive machines, those who trade and construct armaments, the lawmakers in Washington, and ourselves who are blinded to this helpless, ongoing agony.

Ignatius, in his meditation on the First Degree of Humility, asks us to be aware of our reaction in the face of these forces of violence. Are we willing to sacrifice our own livelihood rather than be passive cooperators in the death of others?

This First Degree is very difficult, for though evil in itself has no appeal, the fringe benefits and the profits are enormously attractive. Persons trained to obey in the military need great understanding and compassion when they transfer from a life of violence to a life of peace.

Would I give my life rather than make the tools of war? Would you? Would I be able to give up honors, prestige and employment? Would you?

The offering of the First Degree of Humility requires the grace of understanding and the courage to act.

2 TIMOTHY 4:6, 8 AS FOR ME, MY LIFE IS ALREADY BEING POURED AWAY AS A LIBATION, AND THE TIME HAS COME FOR ME TO BE GONE. I HAVE FOUGHT THE GOOD FIGHT TO THE END; I HAVE RUN THE RACE TO THE FINISH; I HAVE KEPT THE FAITH.

77. IN THE WORLD BUT NOT OF IT

When Ignatius spoke of the Second Degree of Humility in his Spiritual Exercises, he presumed that the retreatant would have a great sense of awareness. The person making the Exercises must be acquainted with the subtleties of society and the complexities of his own nature.

Since each person's freedom is limited, the degree of accountability and culpability is relative. When a person looks at the effects, he does not readily see the cause.

In this Second Degree, we are asked to study the elements that cause mistrust and hatred. Ignatius wants us to observe the fears and worries that lead to non-reflective, compulsive behavior. He asks us to realize how vulnerable we were and how easily we have been manipulated. For example, past beliefs are so ingrained that no matter how convincing the argument, no matter how clear the facts, our habitual way of seeing makes us almost incapable of changing.

Ignatius reminds us how natural it is for the conditioned person to have resentments and for a most gifted person to feel rejected. At times we are tempted to curse the darkness and condemn the world.

In the Second Degree of Humility, Ignatius wants us to see the world with its limitations and ourselves with our inhibitions. Can we accept these limitations in nature, in people, in ourselves? This is the matter God has given us to work with. This is the clay and the milieu.

What you see is what you are. How would you like to reshape what God has created?

Ignatius wanted us to discover that the world is still in process. We have enormous resources to satisfy our desires and the needs of others.

When the people outside our door are starving, the meal we are having loses its flavor. We can put up walls, close doors or create some distance between them and us, but sooner or later we will see them, for we are related and our paths will cross. Sharing our gifts, rather than harboring resentments toward those who cause injustice, is the true work of justice.

When we believe that God accepts us eternally and unequivocally, it makes it easier. Once we understand that, we actually return acceptance in exchange for rejections received. We can forgive prayerfully and carefully, as we ourselves take the initiative.

We discover the kind of nourishment a person needs to bear fruit, and we offer the appropriate attention, affection and assurance.

Ignatius requests that we live our lives in a humble way, while working for justice and peace. This blest work gives great consolation and diffuses God's goodness to many corners of the land. This Grace of the Second Degree of Humility defuses the power of greed and violence and infuses generosity and peace.

MATTHEW 25:44, 45 "LORD, WHEN DID WE SEE YOU HUNGRY OR THIRSTY, A STRANGER OR NAKED, SICK OR IN PRISON, AND DID NOT COME TO YOUR HELP?" THEN HE WILL ANSWER, "I TELL YOU SOLEMNLY, IN SO FAR AS YOU NEGLECTED TO DO THIS TO ONE OF THE LEAST OF THESE, YOU NEGLECTED TO DO IT TO ME."

78. DISCOVERING OUR DESIRE FOR CHRIST

When Ignatius speaks of the Third Degree of Humility, he asks if the retreatant would prefer to be poor with Christ poor, rejected with Christ rejected and considered to be a fool with Christ rather than have any worldly honor apart from Christ.

Who would ever desire to be poor, sick and rejected? All things being equal, who would ever aspire to these evils of the world? Ignatius is not actually asking us to go against our nature, for our whole nature hungers to be healthy and accepted. Ignatius wanted us to discover how important our desires were, so that we would be like Christ who knew what He wanted.

Sometimes when we think we would like to be rich we can ask ourselves, "Would I rather be rich, or poor with Christ who is poor? A simpler formula is, "Would I prefer to be rich, or happy?" This meditation is not a focus on material objects, but a centering on our priority to be with Christ under all conditions.

When a child is sick, the mother finds herself praying, "Dear God, give me the sickness, don't let my child suffer." This is love of the Third Degree: wanting to be sick with those you love, to wish to be poor with those you love, and willing, even preferring to be rejected or considered a fool with those you love.

It seems like such an obvious choice to walk with Christ, rejected and abused, rather than to sit in the place of Caiaphas, Herod or Pilate.

We have the poor, the sick and the rejected near us always. Can we understand and feel compassion for the rejected? Do we sense our spiritual oneness and brotherhood? Do we realize that those who are imprisoned are our brothers and sisters? This Third Degree of Humility is one of great awareness and clear perception. Pride, glory and the riches of society fade when we feel Christ's presence and love.

This is the true grace of prayer, seeing Christ in each person. We find ourselves loving without embarrassment as though every person were Christ, which he is, and as though you were Christ loving each one, which you are. Nothing can keep us from seeing Christ in each person.

JOHN 1:50, 51 JESUS REPLIED, "YOU BELIEVE JUST BECAUSE I SAID: I SAW YOU UNDER THE FIG TREE? YOU WILL SEE GREATER THINGS THAN THAT." AND THEN HE ADDED, "I TELL YOU MOST SOLEMNLY, YOU WILL SEE HEAVEN LAID OPEN AND ABOVE THE SON OF MAN, THE ANGELS OF GOD ASCENDING AND DESCENDING."

Juan Ramón Moreno Pardo, S.J.
29 August 1933 - 16 November 1989

Amando Lopez Quintana, S.J.
6 February 1936 - 16 November 1989

79. A POLITICAL PRAYER

I pray today for those elected officials in public office who are giving their lives to serve and to protect the human rights of the underprivileged, the uneducated, the homeless and the elderly sick. I pray especially for those who, while not being elected by the poor, are willing to serve them.

I also pray that governments that promote imperialism, violence and weapons' production and proliferation will be subdued by the cries and tears of witnesses for peace. It will certainly require a miracle, for those who lobby for weapons get great wealth allocated to them. They obtain enormous military contracts and in a very direct way, these officials export suffering and terror.

This lethal triangle, the monetary, the military and the political, can only be overcome by the good will of brave people, by their intelligent voices and by their sincere prayerfulness. Compassionate civilians represented by a fearless press are the only conscience for a conspiracy of such magnitude.

I pray also for another miracle. The crimes of these so-called authorities have been against humanity. They wage war against neighboring poor countries defacing the principles of democracy: peace, freedom and the pursuit of happiness.

I pray that our reputation as a people who are generous with their resources and resourceful with their generosity can be restored. Prayer leads to action when we write or call our elected officials. Our prayer leads to caring and our caring needs expression. This would be one clear signal that not only the Press is awake but that the electorate is speaking out.

ACTS 4:31 AS THEY PRAYED, THE HOUSE WHERE THEY WERE ASSEMBLED ROCKED; THEY WERE ALL FILLED WITH THE HOLY SPIRIT AND BEGAN TO PROCLAIM THE WORD OF GOD BOLDLY.

80. I AM THE RESURRECTION AND THE LIFE

When did the resurrection of Jesus become significant to you? When you first heard it, were you concerned about a life after this life? Was it taught to you as a doctrine to be accepted as though it were an obvious fact about the future?

When you heard, "Unless the grain of wheat dies, it cannot flourish," did this text cause you to question the value of life? Words have the power to manipulate your feelings, to excite, console or depress you.

When did Benigno Aquino, Anwar Sadat, Oscar Romero and the Sisters and Priests from El Salvador rise from the dead? Is resurrection on the last day only?

Have you met people who are risen already? Certain people are resurrected every day of their lives, while others get stuck on the word, "Resurrection," as though it were some future event. They keep staring at the revered signpost while missing the path and the people who live on the street. They profess the outward sign but miss life.

Jesus said, "I am the Resurrection" and "You and I are one." Do you believe that as Jesus is the Resurrection you are also?

Dorothy, Ita, Jean and Maura, the dedicated women martyrs of El Salvador were filled with life before they died. Their life did not end. They did not need another resurrection. Romero, before he died at the altar, and Aquino, before he died at the airport, had risen to new life. Cory Aquino, still working for peace has already risen.

Jesus loved to wake people up. Jesus wants us to wake up, to rise up to this new life. One of the loveliest signs that you have awakened, that you have resurrected is that you can look back and laugh at your empty tomb. Your tomb is not some place to which you are going, it is a place from which you have come.

When you are unafraid of life, you can no longer be manipulated by your conscience, by authority or by what people might think. You will feel the resurrection and the life.

Jesus came that you might have life! Do not let anyone take your life away from you and do not let life pass you by.

*JOHN 6: 47, 48 I TELL YOU MOST SOLEMNLY, EVERY-
BODY WHO BELIEVES HAS ETERNAL LIFE. I AM THE
BREAD OF LIFE.*

Ignacio Martin Baró, S.J.
7 November 1942 - 16 November 1989

Ignacio Ellacuria, S.J.
9 November 1930 - 16 November 1989

81. YOUR HAPPINESS IS MY DESIRE

The One who loves you says, *"I want your joy to be complete. I want you to be at peace so that your heart is not troubled and you are not anxious. My own joy is complete, for I have you in the palm of My hands and you are always in My presence. Since I want very much for you to be happy, may I help you today in any way? Are there some desires that you need to be fulfilled? Are there some wishes that you would like granted? Are there some hopes that you would like to see realized? Is there some satisfaction that you still hunger for? Are you seeking a joy greater than you already have? Could you clarify these desires to yourself and would you spell them out for Me?*

You will notice as you list the things that you hope for, that some of them are not yours. Some of these things do not come from your heart. Often your desires come from outside, maybe from others, maybe from voices of the past. If only you could locate your authentic desires you would find Me in each one. You would experience peace and joy and great satisfaction.

When you searched for Me, sometimes you did not find Me. Remember? How could you ever find Me when you and I are one, when I am in you and you are in Me?

What I want for you is that you enjoy life to the full. And so your desires are my desires, and your wishes are my wishes, and your hopes are my hopes, and your satisfaction is my satisfaction. Does this surprise you? Does this please you?

I want you to know with absolute certainty that you and I have always been one in heart, in spirit, in life and in love. Doesn't that amaze you when you look back at the past and realize we were never apart? Nothing has ever separated us and nothing ever could.

What makes our journey a joy is that we are searching together. Compared with any exploration of the past, the pilgrimage we have taken together has had greater significance.

Far more than any peace that you could find in the world, the peace that I have with you is incomparable. And I know it will make your heart dance when you realize that during your entire life you have given Me ineffable joy.

With every breath and step that you took, I rejoiced. My satisfaction is complete. I pray for you this day, that whatever you do, wherever you go, whatever you say and feel, that your joy may be complete as well."

JOHN 15:7, 9 IF YOU REMAIN IN ME AND MY WORDS REMAIN IN YOU, ASK WHAT YOU WILL AND YOU SHALL GET IT. AS THE FATHER HAS LOVED ME, SO I HAVE LOVED YOU. REMAIN IN MY LOVE.

Joaquin Lopez Y Lopez, S.J
16 August 1918 - 16 November 1989

Segundo Montes Mozo, S.J.
15 may 1933 - 16 November 1989

82. GOD IS FOND OF YOU

Many people are more aware of the past than of the present. The present is too unpredictable and too dynamic. Therefore, people tend to focus much of their life on the static past, whether distant or recent.

Since God lives in the now, creating these very moments, the present is a great resource for discovering the living God. But God is very hard to find even in the present, for God is utter and complete mystery.

Can you picture the Lord saying: *"I created this day just for you. Today is a holy day because I created it and because it is wholly yours. Every day is a Sabbath day, a singularly special day. I don't need days Myself; I made them for you. I enjoyed creating today for you and I am fully happy with what I created. It is my gift to you.*

There is something unusual about this gift. I'd like you to notice that there are no strings. I have created this day with no "ifs". Don't consider, please, any right or wrong, any right way of acting, or any right way of seeing. Any way you breathe, any manner in which you live is absolutely fine with Me. And the way you see life, it might seem human to you, but it is divine with Me.

While you were resting last night, I was reflecting whether you could please me if you acted a certain way today. I realized I have no particular will for you. You don't have to guess my mind! There were no conditions for today; there were no expectations at all. Today is pure gift.

I like you just the way I made you. Sometimes I would like you to see the things that I see and sometimes I would like you to see things the way I do. But then you would be Me. And I really enjoy the things you see and the way you see them. And I like you the way you are.

It is most important to Me that you are you. I get a heavenly charge out of your feelings and the unusual things you worry about and your silly plans. You are so different. I am really delighted with you.

Remember how you enjoyed watching a little child at sleep or play? I'm like that too. I never get tired watching you sleep. And I love it when you play. I love being aware of you. I am eternally happy Myself and I love seeing you happy.

Good morning to you! There is so much you can be aware of today; and whatever you choose, I am with you, and whatever you discover, I rejoice with you."

TITUS 3:4, 7 WHEN THE KINDNESS AND LOVE OF GOD OUR SAVIOR WERE REVEALED, IT WAS NOT BECAUSE HE WAS CONCERNED WITH ANY RIGHTEOUS ACTIONS WE MIGHT HAVE DONE OURSELVES; IT WAS FOR NO REASON EXCEPT HIS OWN COMPASSION THAT HE SAVED US. HE DID THIS SO THAT WE SHOULD BE JUSTIFIED BY HIS GRACE, TO BECOME HEIRS LOOKING FORWARD TO INHERITING ETERNAL LIFE. THIS IS DOCTRINE THAT YOU CAN RELY ON.

83. I AM WITH YOU

Let the Lord speak... *"I am closer to you than you are to yourself. Is it hard for you to understand this? Words cannot describe, hearts cannot express our oneness, our fullness. It is simply true.*

If you could remember all the breaths you have breathed, if you could even now feel the air that touches your face and hands, you would get some sense of our closeness.

If you could recall all the things you have seen, all the colors and shapes, all things near and far, things simple and dramatic, all the words you have heard, all the sounds since childhood, you would know that I have always been with you. You and I have always been intimately together; nothing could separate us.

When you no longer see and hear, still I am with you. When you try to turn away from me, I sometimes turn you around, and sometimes I come around Myself, but usually I just hide more deeply within you.

From the first moment of your existence, you and I have been one. Nothing you or anyone else might have done could ever separate us. Nothing in all of life could ever come between us. Even death has no power to separate us, even for a second.

You have no reason ever again to be threatened, to be afraid, to be anxious, for you are Mine and I am yours.

I am closer to you than you are to yourself."

ROMANS 8:38, 39 FOR I AM CERTAIN OF THIS: NEITHER DEATH NOR LIFE, NO ANGEL, NO PRINCE, NOTHING THAT EXISTS, NOTHING STILL TO COME, NOT ANY POWER, OR HEIGHT OR DEPTH, NOR ANY CREATED THING, CAN EVER COME BETWEEN US AND THE LOVE OF GOD MADE VISIBLE IN CHRIST JESUS OUR LORD.

84. STORMY DAYS

The thunder drew my attention today; it always does. It makes me look for the flashes of light in the sky. It makes me wonder how far away the lightning is and in which direction the storm is moving. Hopefully, away from here!

As I was waiting for the next thunderclap, I thought of other places that have light and noises in the sky that are more terrifying. I thought of the rockets exploding over the huddled refugees in Tyre and Sidon.

The powerful cracking sounds of nature do damage but they are not intended to maim, to violate or to terrorize God's people. Nature, while violent is not revengeful.

I looked at the rain coming down with splash landings and at the little puddles that formed. When surrounded by stormy weather and lightning, I tend to look for a dry and protected place to observe these forces of nature. It is natural to be excited by the flashes of light and the unusual sounds.

God reminds us in so many ways to examine life and to be aware of other people and what they are enduring. With every sound and sight, and with every thought and feeling, the Lord whispers, *"Be not afraid. I have created all this and I have created you. All these things are mine. All those poor huddled refugees in the Middle East are mine. And you are too. So do not be afraid of anything in life, for nothing can wrest you from my arms. Nothing can wrest you from my love. So be in awe, if you will, of the great sounds in the sky, but be not afraid. And of all the things that you do or say and of all the things that you see and hear, be in awe, if you will, but be not afraid.*

Now listen to the thunder. Hold your ears if you must. Look at the lightning. Enjoy the raindrops today."

MARK 4:41 "WHY ARE YOU SO FRIGHTENED? HOW IS IT THAT YOU HAVE NO FAITH?" THEY WERE FILLED WITH AWE AND SAID TO ONE ANOTHER, "WHO CAN THIS BE? EVEN THE WIND AND THE SEA OBEY HIM."

85. WE ARE INSEPARABLE

Be very quiet and listen to these words.

"Without Me you can do nothing. That is true. But, of course, you are never without Me. I am always with you. You and I can never be separated even for a moment under any condition.

Who told you that you could be away from Me or separated from Me or apart from Me? Can you remember the very first time you believed that we were distant from each other? Can you recall the first time you suspected that maybe I did not love you with all of My heart? Can you remember the situation or the person that convinced you to doubt My eternal affection for you?

The only reason that you need these encouraging words, 'I am with you' is because at some point in your life you thought I might be away from you. Someone misled you to believe that I might abandon you, or withhold My love from you.

You never doubted My love when you were a child. Little children think that nothing is impossible with Me. Aware religious would never threaten little children with the loss of My love - not even to control their behavior. Understanding parents would certainly not threaten their own children with being separated from their Creator!

And so, whoever convinced you that it was possible to be separated from Me was either very ignorant or severely indoctrinated. I can assure you, he was not convinced of My love for him, so how could he announce My love to you?

You can walk with confidence and curiosity because you know that wherever you stray or wherever you stay you will find Me. You can be daringly you, because no matter what decision you make, you will please Me. Even if you make no effort at all, your breath, your heartbeat, your thoughts and your feelings are from Me. Little children already realize this. They are accustomed to people smiling at them, caring for their needs and making them feel secure. Those who need to be reminded that I love them eternally and unconditionally are those who were taught that it was possible for Me to be absent from them. It is okay for you to ask for signs of assurance; just ask with the freedom of a child.

Now you know that nothing can separate you and Me. Maybe now you can accept yourself and the limitations of others. Accepting of your successes and failures, you will appreciate equally criticism or praise. Once you are fully aware of my love for you nothing will seem overwhelming. You will find many more miracles occurring in your life.

Because of the assurance of my active presence and love, you will become more sensitive and less threatened. When you are challenged, confronted or overlooked, you will not be bothered. In fact you will rejoice, for you are certain that nothing is impossible for you and Me."

1 PETER 1:8, 9 YOU DID NOT SEE HIM, YET YOU LOVE HIM; AND STILL WITHOUT SEEING HIM, YOU ARE ALREADY FILLED WITH A JOY SO GLORIOUS THAT IT CANNOT BE DESCRIBED, BECAUSE YOU BELIEVE; AND YOU ARE SURE OF THE END TO WHICH YOUR FAITH LOOKS FORWARD, THAT IS, THE SALVATION OF YOUR SOULS.

86. YOU ARE A MIRACLE

Be still and listen to the Lord.

"I just could not wait for you to wake up this morning. I stirred some clouds and wondered if you would hear the sounds and wake up. I love you so.

While I am pleasantly ecstatic seeing you sleep, I enjoy your rising and those first thoughts that come to your mind. It is fun to watch your tired mind and body make its first movements of the day. It is so amazing how your body functions, the billions of cells, each doing its living thing!

You are so incapable of being aware of all but a few movements of your body. I guess you will never know how completely happy I am with your body: its creaks and circulation, its sensitivity to air and water, its varied response to objects that it sees or touches. I think it is great that you are so nonchalant about your fine tuned organism.

What I like too, is your communication system, the signals that your body gives your head, that your mind gives your heart and then relays to your body. When you ask your body to respond, it usually obeys instantly. You do so many things unconsciously even though you appear to be aware. I find it amusing when you concentrate on something and your whole energy is focused. And I love you.

Did you enjoy the comfort of sleep with the sheet over your shoulder? Did you like the stimulation of waking? Did you enjoy the freedom of thinking, seeing and moving around? I happen to like you whether you are at rest or fully active. I see you as a world unto yourself, so filled with life. You are like a unique planet poised in a special place. You are independent from every other created planet. You have your own space and atmosphere surrounding you. And I love you.

You move in your own orbit and you twirl at your own pace. You have your own life. As you reflect the light, you reveal many different shades and shapes. You are a world that gives rest and stimulation to those who come your way. Sometimes you are passive and quiet - you live and let others be. You are very much like Me. I live and let others be also.

As you walk in the light, sometimes you absorb it. At other times you block it and cast lovely shadows. Sometimes you share light and shade with others. And I love you.

Sometimes you are very active and vivacious, at others, very un-selfconscious. You seem to have discovered you are okay. You seem to enjoy your own being, your own existence, your own unusual essence. You seem to be satisfied with the space around you and the varying degrees of light. You seem to accept your own activity and inactivity with all its variables. And when you meet others, you are not envious. Me, neither. I am able to enjoy people and they can enjoy Me. You can enjoy them, and they certainly enjoy you.

We can see each other, we can share with each other, we can affect each other and still be ourselves. We do not have to become something we are not.

Do you love yourself immensely? I do. Are you growing in appreciation of the things I have created? Do you find yourself accepting the other centers that revolve around you? I take great delight in you and in those around you.

I love you so."

THE SONG OF SONGS 2:4 IN HIS LONGED-FOR SHADE I AM SEATED AND HIS FRUIT IS SWEET TO MY TASTE. HE HAS TAKEN ME TO HIS BANQUET HALL, AND THE BANNER HE RAISES OVER ME IS LOVE.

87. PEACE MEANS LOVING YOUR NEIGHBOR

How often do you see your neighbor as yourself? Here are a few questions to help you discover whether you have been influenced by the pressure of society to become other than God made you. How many people in your surroundings with different political or religious beliefs from your own, do you see as yourself? Recently, when did you love your neighbor as you loved yourself? When did you treat your neighbor as you would like to be treated? How can you tell if you are a person of peace? How can you tell if you love your neighbor? How often do you find yourself striving for the prize, struggling to be the victor, or straining for the reward?

In order to have peace, you must choose cooperation over competition. You must give up judging. To the degree that you desire true peace, you must resolve internal conflicts. If you desire peace, there are certain things that cannot co-exist. A person who speaks of peace and who is working for peace must renounce all violence.

In our society, we hear of groups, companies, churches and nations desiring to dominate and be the largest.

After hearing Jesus say, "Love your neighbor as yourself," why would anyone want to defeat his neighbor? Where does that motivation come from that compels a person to conquer others or to condemn himself? What is the prize that induces people to strive for victory and honor rather than to live in peace?

Some people find their joy in relating, sharing, working and playing. They find their joy in peaceful things. Others aspire to a different life-style as they strive to become something else or someone else. They not only wish the world would change, but they also make efforts to change the world. These people are seldom satisfied, for they know there is so much more they could change in themselves. However, their efforts are misguided. Somehow they have been taught that victory, conquering, being the best or being above the rest is more important than harmony, acceptance and peace. They believe that becoming more than they are is better than being who they are.

These driven people feel that being above others is better than being one among many equals and that converting others is more important than accepting others. Religious fanatics feel they must win the Kingdom, for they do not see it all around them. They do not realize that the Kingdom already belongs to others and them. If the righteous could see the source of their indoctrination and programming, their hearts would be opened. They would rejoice and realize that it is not really necessary to be bigger than any other person, church or nation. Their hearts would be at rest. They would love their near and far neighbors and they would be able to find God in all things.

Blessed are the peacemakers, for they see God.

LUKE 4:18, 19 THE SPIRIT OF THE LORD HAS BEEN GIVEN TO ME. HE HAS SENT ME TO BRING THE GOOD NEWS TO THE POOR, TO PROCLAIM LIBERTY TO CAPTIVES, TO SET THE DOWNTRODDEN FREE, TO PROCLAIM THE LORD'S YEAR OF FAVOR.

88. MY PEACE I GIVE TO YOU

Peace involves powerlessness, which we certainly had during the early stages of childhood and which we certainly have at the end of our lives.

We were accepted into the body of our mother and we have been received by the family of our childhood. We have been received by the world and we have been accepted by God. With all this acceptance we still hunger for expressions of recognition. We co-exist with every other human being and we have the same right to exist as every other being. We take up a certain amount of space and time, and so does every other creation. From the first moment of our life and at our last, we are equal with all beings in creation. And we can never lose that equality.

However there exists a high degree of insecurity. We are incapable of clinging to life. How insecure we truly are! The security we do have is contained in the mysterious love of God. Nothing is more secure in life than knowing that God loves us unconditionally. What distracts us from flourishing with this peaceful notion?

We desire a sense of integration with our own thoughts and feelings and desires. We desire to be in harmony with everything that God has created. Before our first breath, we have been one with creation and during our life we have been intimately associated with beings that God has created.

Many have been programmed to believe that those who have power are better than the powerless. Many more have been conditioned to think that peace comes through power and violence. Pity is all that is offered for the losers and the victims!

Society has told us that we are not one and that we are not at peace with one another and that we should not expect it. Society taught people to compete, confront and, if necessary to conflict. "Victory" became the standard rather than "Peace." We must conquer the others, convert others, achieve our goals and become winners. Many influences not just economic, religious, political and athletic - sway us to be superior. We were told that victory could be attained by overwhelming resources and power. Deep within we have this powerlessness, yet we were taught to overcome it. This illusion of victory attained by being superior to others is a major obstacle to peace.

Jesus encouraged us to believe in peace and to be makers of peace. He has given us His peace to start with, a peace which the world cannot earn by victory. He encouraged us by saying He had already conquered the world.

His peace belongs to all of us. It is your gift.

JOHN 20:20 - 22 JESUS CAME AND STOOD AMONG THEM. HE SAID TO THEM, "PEACE BE WITH YOU," AND SHOWED THEM HIS HANDS AND HIS SIDE. THE DISCIPLES WERE FILLED WITH JOY WHEN THEY SAW THE LORD, AND HE SAID TO THEM AGAIN, "PEACE BE WITH YOU. AS THE FATHER SENT ME, SO AM I SENDING YOU." AFTER SAYING THIS HE BREATHED ON THEM AND SAID: "RECEIVE THE HOLY SPIRIT."

89. WE DO NOT KNOW THE WAY

When you know the way, you may be filled with confidence, but routine can stifle your joy.

Have you noticed the feeling you get when you do not know the way? How natural it is to be worried and anxious, for there are so many things we do not know. We do not know the outcome of today nor the far reaching effects of yesterday. We do not know the future, nor the length of our years. How can we make valid plans when we do not know the effects of our actions? The truth is, we are living more in mystery than we are in certainty.

Have you ever watched little children playing in a park which they had never visited before? They bring their confidence with them as they walk the unfamiliar paths. You have to wonder at their audacity, for they are so willing to experiment, to be daring, even apparently, to get lost. I smile when I see their unpredictable approach to the world.

Do you feel that you view life courageously? Do you find yourself enjoying the unknown as well as the known? There is so much to see. The world is mysterious and you yourself are incarnate mystery. In each step you take, you are walking in mystery. Your mind and senses that connect you to the world are replete with mystery.

When you have lived many years how can you treat this one day as though it were brand new, as though you do not know it at all? How does a person make this moment of creation special?

How do you sense the wonder of the world deeply? First, admit that you know and you do not know. Every person you have talked to or listened to, every preacher or teacher that has ever spoken, knows and does not know. With their natural limitations they have shared the best they could. You must also. But at the outset realize you do not know the way.

Second, admit honestly that no one knows the way and no one ever knew the way. You will then not raise up false gods of a national, religious or personal nature. You will find yourself less idealistic but more gentle in accepting yourself and others. You will rejoice in your understanding and perception without striving to grasp it all and without straining to know it all.

Finally, once you are comfortable with mystery, you will find yourself saying in more situations, "How curious, how marvelous! And I don't even know the way."

MARK 9:37 "ANYONE WHO WELCOMES ONE OF THESE LITTLE CHILDREN IN MY NAME, WELCOMES ME; AND ANYONE WHO WELCOMES ME WELCOMES THE ONE WHO SENT ME."

90. GOD CREATES LIFE FOR OUR ENJOYMENT

If you tried to list all the people and events that brought joy to your life, where would you start? You might recall your childhood and the people who were your companions over the years. There were certain reunions that were happy occasions. Was it observing nature, accomplishing personal projects, or relating to people that was the most constant source of joy? Have you become more conscious of the things that bring you satisfaction?

How much joy do you receive from a child who likes you and who spends time with you? Can you measure that joy? Think of some friends and how much joy you received by their presence and communication. Did you feel that natural desire to cling and later sense a desire to let go?

Think of the different times you were alone. Were you able to sense the joy of independence, of working, of deciding for yourself? Were you aware of the moments of fullness and the desire to move on?

When you looked at nature were your senses filled; and were you satisfied again? The fullness includes the taking in, letting it be and then letting it flow. You are God's creation passing through life, and it is up to you to find joy in the present moment.

How much did you enjoy the walk? Did you enjoy your room, looking around, rearranging things and putting them in place? Did you enjoy lying down and rising? Did you enjoy every moment?

If you are not enjoying every observation, activity and exchange, find the possible reasons for your not enjoying each moment.

Some who think that joy is in the future are always preparing for some elusive drama. Those who think that joy was in the past are desperately trying to preserve their memories. Those who feel they are deprived get caught up in jealousy and envy at the possessions and joys of others.

Joy is the discovery of something that is being created this moment. It is a realization rather than an accomplishment. And like each second of life it passes on and does not return. New seconds keep occurring. This is the strange way that God has created human joy. Joy is as intimate as our breathing and as plentiful as air.

We celebrate the arrival of new life, the miraculous transition from mystery to life. And we celebrate death, the departure of life, the transition from life to mystery. In between, there is time for a billion feelings, a million activities, ten thousand faces and places.

How much joy does a child give you? How much joy can your heart contain? How much joy do you receive with the acceptance and love of another? How much joy do you receive from appreciating nature and from choosing your daily activities?

Joy appears, overflows and goes. Are you ready for more? God creates it anew every moment.

LUKE 24:51, 52 NOW AS HE BLESSED THEM, HE WITHDREW FROM THEM AND WAS CARRIED UP TO HEAVEN. THEY WORSHIPED HIM AND THEN WENT BACK TO JERUSALEM FULL OF JOY.

91. MANY LITTLE JOYS

When you grasp the joy a child has, you appreciate your vocation; for yours is the same.

How great is the joy of a child walking, sitting down to eat, reading a story with you, standing on her head with her feet still on the floor?

A vocation is not a call from the past, nor a call to some future achievement, but a call to live today, sometimes walking or riding, sometimes sitting at table with a friend, sometimes standing on your head with your feet on the ground.

If we picked up a child and put her in another room, she would find a way of adjusting to the change. If we replaced one toy with another, or one item of food with another, she would adjust. So can you. You have the ability to find newness in every circumstance.

How do you lose the joy of the moment, the joy of so many things that happen each day? Why aren't you joyful all the time? Did someone tell you you were not supposed to be? Were you taught not to laugh or be happy in class, and that you definitely should not be happy in church? Were you told that there were certain times and places where joy was inappropriate?

Can you remember people who constantly expected more of you? Rather than enjoy your presence they made it their business to criticize what you were doing. To restrict your indomitable spirit took some pretty strong personalities.

Have you met people whose style you found to be a cause of great joy? You seemed to fully appreciate the way they perceived and acted. Fortunately, there were people who enjoyed everything you did and said and who did not try to change you. They were delighted to be in your company. It is refreshing to be with people who cherish you. Today as you stand on your head with your feet on the ground, enjoy certain people who appreciate you and whom you appreciate.

Just as all life has its unique moments and moves, your rhythm is even more miraculous. Have you appreciated the uniqueness of your life?

ACTS 2:17 IN THE DAYS TO COME - IT IS THE LORD WHO SPEAKS - I WILL POUR OUT MY SPIRIT ON ALL MANKIND. THEIR SONS AND DAUGHTERS SHALL PROPHESY, SEE VISIONS, DREAM DREAMS.

Anthony DeMello, SJ & Jim Dolan, SJ with the Sadhana class.

AFTER WORD

Meditations For Life has as its purpose the giving of some insights into spiritual freedom in the same manner that a retreat would provide.

God's love for you is the constant theme of these reflections, because it is the source of your life and freedom.

I hope that each reader will feel singularly loved.

People are confronted throughout life with pressures and illusions that challenge their early belief in God's universal care. I hope people will not be deterred from believing in God's love because of literal interpretations and the fragile ministers of The Good News.

May people burdened by righteous thoughts become more tolerant of the discrepancies between God's love and others' limitations. May those with private fears and personal failures be encouraged by the daily miracles which God reveals. Judgment, fear and guilt all belong to the world, not to God.

Children prance their merry way, naturally loving and thoroughly selfish. Their yeses and noes are transparent and disarming. You are God's child, naturally selfish, yet totally loved and accepted by the Lord.

The responsibility of the Church, the People of God, is to announce Good News. The Good News is still hard to believe and even harder to practice.

So let us find ever new ways to encourage one another.

REVELATION 22:21 MAY THE GRACE OF THE LORD JESUS BE WITH YOU ALL.